A STEADFAST HEART

EXPERIENCING GOD'S COMFORT IN LIFE'S STORMS

Elyse FITZPATRICK

P&R
PUBLISH'
P.O. BOX 817 • PHILLIPSBURG • NEW JERSEY

Unless otherwise indicated, Scripture quotations are from the NEW AMERICAN STANDARD BIBLE®. Copyright © 1960, 1962, 1963, 1968, 1971, 1972, 1973, 1975, 1977, 1995 by The Lockman Foundation. Used by permission.

Scripture quotations marked (esv) are from The Holy Bible, English Standard Version, copyright © 2001 by Crossway Bibles, a division of Good News Publishers. Used by permission. All rights reserved.

Scripture quotations marked (amp) are from the AMPLIFIED BIBLE. Copyright © 1954, 1958, 1962, 1964, 1965, 1987 by The Lockman Foundation, La Habra, CA 90631. All rights reserved. www.lockman.org.

Scripture quotations marked (tlb) are from THE LIVING BIBLE. Copyright © 1971. Used by permission of Tyndale House Publishers, Inc., Wheaton, IL 60189. All rights reserved.

"Christ Shares His People's Sorrows" by Faith Cook from *Grace in Winter: Rutherford in Verse*. Copyright © 1989 by Banner of Truth Trust, Carlisle, Pa. All rights reserved. Used by permission.

"No Scar" by Amy Carmichael from *Toward Jerusalem*. ©1997 by Dohnavur Fellowship, and published by CLC Publications, Fort Washington, PA. All rights reserved. Used by permission.

"God Reigns in the Storm" and "Be Still and Know" written by Steve and Vikki Cook. Copyright 2006 by Before the Throne Music (ASCAP). Taken from the CD "Before the Throne" by Steve and Vikki Cook. For more information on this recording or the ministry of Steve and Vikki Cook please visit www.BeforeTheThroneMusic.com. Before the Throne Music was created to provide cross-centered songs for churches and worshipers..

Page design and typesetting by Lakeside Design Plus

Printed in the United States of America

Library of Congress Cataloging-in-Publication Data

Fitzpatrick, Elyse, 1950–
 A steadfast heart : experiencing God's comfort in life's storms / Elyse Fitzpatrick.
  p. cm.
 Includes bibliographical references.
 ISBN-10: 0-87552-747-7 (paper)
 ISBN-13: 978-0-87552-747-5 (paper)
 1. Bible. O.T. Psalm LVII—Criticism, interpretation, etc. I. Title

BS1450 57th .F58 2006
248.8'6—dc22   2006043287

In memory of
Richard Lewis Pascoe
August 1981–November 2003
"We Believe"

Contents

Acknowledgments

A book like this would never have made it out of my heart and into your hands without the faithful support, help, and persevering prayer of so many people. Women who had heard of the trial Phil and I were facing, and who had perhaps never even met me, let me know of their prayers. Thank you, dear sisters.

Our church (Grace Church of Rancho Bernardo, California) continually surrounded us in prayer, particularly our pastors, Craig Cabannis (now pastoring in North Dallas), Mark Lauterbach, Dan Wilson, and Eric Turbedsky. Our home group prayed consistently and fervently for us and would remind us that they were doing so. We know that God is sovereign, but we also know that God uses means. Thank you for being the means He used to sustain our souls and ultimately deliver us. You humble us and make us thankful.

Thanks go to Pastor Steve Shank, who preached a message on Psalm 57 and the perseverance of the saints to our Sovereign

Grace Small Group Leader's Conference in 2003. That message fed my soul and was the genesis of this book. Thank you for your faithful preaching of God's Word.

I'm sure that readers have already tasted the melody and lyrics that Steve and Vikki Cook have written. It's been my privilege to work with such godly and gifted saints, and to sing their songs week after week in our church. Thanks so much for making this book more than a book—you've made it a gift.

During our difficult time of trial, Phil and I were immensely encouraged by our family: by our children and their spouses, James and Michele, Jessica and Cody, Joel and Ruth. We were particularly encouraged when we had the joy of spending time with our little darlings: Wesley, Hayden, Eowyn, and Allie. These little rays of sunshine in a beclouded sky fed our souls and gave us hope. Thank you for loving us and letting us love you.

My most sincere gratitude goes to Phil, my faithful husband. During our entire trial, he consistently conducted himself with integrity, honor, faith, and grace. It was primarily because of his example and his consistent prayer and love that I was able to make it through some of the darkest times. Thank you, dearest.

Thanks also to my dear friends at P&R, particularly Barbara Lerch, who encouraged my writing of this, and Tara Davis, who edited the manuscript and had to patiently chase down all my loose ends.

> Be exalted, O God, above the heavens!
> Let your glory be over all the earth! (Ps. 57:11 esv)

Before You Read This Book

The beloved disciple gazed forward into heaven from his lonely exile on Patmos and wrote:

> For the Lamb in the midst of the throne will be
>   their shepherd,
>   and he will guide them to springs of living water,
>   and God will wipe away every tear from their
>   eyes. (Rev. 7:17 ESV)

He will wipe away every tear from their eyes, and death shall be no more, neither shall there be mourning nor crying nor pain anymore, for the former things have passed away. (Rev. 21:4 ESV)

Although the days of freedom from mourning, crying, and pain are our future hope, it may be that the storm you're presently experiencing is so battering your soul that you find it hard to read, and the thought of trying to learn something new is just too overwhelming right now. Because we're aware of these possibilities, we've recorded a CD for you to listen to—to sing, cry, and pray with. Songwriters Steve and Vikki Cook, through their publishing company, Before the Throne Music, have sought to bring you music that will comfort and edify your soul. We trust that you'll find a safe haven there.

We've also included on the CD several readings from Scripture, a personal message from the author to you, poems from *Grace in Winter: Rutherford in Verse*, by Faith Cook, and prayers from *The Valley of Vision: A Collection of Puritan Prayers and Devotions*.

It is our prayer that you will find grace and strength through the ministry of this CD and that God's Spirit will speak comfort, peace, and blessing to you.

Let Your Glory Be over All the Earth

PSALM 57 (ESV)

*To the choirmaster: according to Do Not Destroy.
A Miktam of David, when he fled from Saul, in the
cave.*

Be merciful to me, O God, be merciful to me,
　　for in you my soul takes refuge;
in the shadow of your wings I will take refuge,
　　till the storms of destruction pass by.
I cry out to God Most High,
　　to God who fulfills his purpose for me.
He will send from heaven and save me;
　　he will put to shame him who tramples on
　　　　me.　　　　　　　　　　　　　　*Selah*
God will send out his steadfast love and his
　　faithfulness!
My soul is in the midst of lions;
　　I lie down amid fiery beasts—
the children of man, whose teeth are spears
　　　　and arrows,
　　whose tongues are sharp swords.
Be exalted, O God, above the heavens!
　　Let your glory be over all the earth!
They set a net for my steps;
　　my soul was bowed down.
They dug a pit in my way,
　　but they have fallen into it themselves.
　　　　　　　　　　　　　　　　　　Selah

My heart is steadfast, O God,
　　my heart is steadfast!

I will sing and make melody!
    Awake, my glory!
Awake, O harp and lyre!
    I will awake the dawn!
I will give thanks to you, O Lord, among the
        peoples;
    I will sing praises to you among the nations.
For your steadfast love is great to the heavens,
    your faithfulness to the clouds.
Be exalted, O God, above the heavens!
    Let your glory be over all the earth!

God Reigns in the Storm

There's a tempest that can flood the soul,
    when troubles pound like crashing waves.
In these afflictions I have realized,
    there's a place that I can hide.
I know that God has promised me His
      strength,
    and His Word can never fail.
He is faithful, O so faithful.

(CHORUS)
There are sovereign hands holding all my
      days.
Yes, I know God reigns in the storm.
Every trial and pain, wisdom has ordained.
Yes, I know God reigns in the storm.

There's a midnight that can fill the soul,
    when the darkness knows no end.
And though it feels like I am all alone,
    there's a truth that gives me hope.
I know the One who's counted all my tears,
    and He is nearer than my breath.
He is with me, always with me.

(CHORUS)

There're so many things that I don't
      understand.
But I know His every plan for me is good, so
      good.

(CHORUS)

He reigns.

Be Still and Know

When mountains fall and waters rise,
    come hide yourself in me.
The One whose voice commands the worlds
    still knows your every need.
Come now and wait on me;
    draw near and rest in me.

(CHORUS)
Be still and know that I am God.
Be still and know that I am God.

When darkness falls and sorrows rise,
    remember who I am.
The One who dwells in eternity,
    still comforts His own child.
Come now and look to me;
    draw near and hope in me.

(CHORUS)

When darkness falls and sorrows rise,
    remember who I am.

—Steve and Vikki Cook

Introduction

A Steadfast Heart:
Experiencing God's Comfort in Life's Storms

What is it about that title that intrigues or interests you? Do you wonder what it means to have a steadfast heart? Do you question whether your heart is steadfast or not? Although discovering what a steadfast heart looks like might be your motivation in picking up this book, I'm supposing that other readers are vitally interested in how to experience God's comfort, right here, right now, in the middle of their personal storm. Perhaps you don't even believe that you can be comforted—it feels like it's been so long since anything resembling comfort was part of your life that you hope you'll be able to glimpse God's face somewhere in this dark and gloomy tempest. Or perhaps you believe that God is comforting you but want to know more about what He's up to. So, whether you're looking for a more steadfast heart, trying to find God's comfort in a storm, or want to spend some time with a sister and Psalm 57 (our primary text for this book), you've come to the right place. In the pages that follow we'll journey together through this divinely inspired prayer, and we'll see how God consoles us. We'll even seek to discover why He brings storms our way (Job 37:9–13). We'll also learn what it means to have a steadfast heart and how a storm surge of joy and worship can burst forth from you in grateful thanks and praise for His steadfast love!

A National Tragedy Becomes Personal

Like most people in America, I spent most of September 11, 2001, glued to the television. I distinctly remember what I felt when I watched those towers come down: confusion, terror, and overwhelming sorrow. I wept.

A little later in the day I received a phone call from a relative informing me that my aged father, who worked in proximity to the World Trade Center, was near the disaster, and, although he was not injured, he was unable to get home. Hours went slowly by, and many prayers were offered until finally, near the end of the day, I heard the good news that he had boarded a tug boat at Battery Park and had been brought uptown to his home. He was well, and though I was filled with grief and sorrow for the thousands of people who had suffered that day, I thought I was safe. I hadn't really been touched . . . or so I thought. Oh, how wrong I was.

I was wrong because, in response to their losses from the 9/11 tragedy, insurance companies modified the way they pay disaster claims. For most people this wouldn't present a major problem, but for my husband, Phil, and me, it did. That's because Phil owned and operated a disaster restoration company that serviced claims from homeowners who had suffered some form of loss: a fire, flood, or vandalism. The lifeblood of our business depended upon insurance companies that were severely affected by the terrorist attacks. In fact, we're still reeling from the aftershocks of that tragic day.

The way that this and other difficulties played out in our lives is that from day to day, Phil and I didn't know whether we were going to make it financially. Because we were the owners of our business, if it failed it meant more than just looking for a new job. It meant the loss of everything we owned. This was the new reality for us.

In addition, along about 2003, I began to experience some strange physical symptoms that have never been conclusively diagnosed. The strain of the difficulties we were facing—Were we going to be able to make our payroll? Were we going to have a house to live in? What would happen to our adult children who worked in the business with us? Would our family be torn apart? What would happen to our grandchildren?—took its toll on my body. I struggled and felt as though a burden had been placed on my back that I couldn't find any escape from. The doctors had a neat little Latin label for this condition but couldn't offer any real help.

As if all this weren't enough, it was in the summer of 2003 that our beloved pastor, Craig Cabaniss, and a number of much-loved families from our church told us that they believed God was calling them to plant a church in north Dallas and that they would be leaving within the year. Every family in our church spent months crying buckets of tears at the rending of such precious relationships.

From 2002 until around March 2005, it seemed that every new day brought a new storm front, a pounding that we hadn't previously known. "You're not going to believe this . . ." was Phil's daily refrain as he came home from work. "They did what?" was my frequent response. Then, when occasionally we hoped we'd seen the proverbial light at the end of the tunnel, we learned that it wasn't relief we'd seen, but rather the 5:00 train from Los Angeles heading straight at us. How long would this go on?

At one point Phil and I found ourselves sitting on a cold bench outside a courtroom. "How did we end up here?" I asked. Until that point, my entire experience with the legal system had included showing up for jury duty and never being selected. As I watched in wonder as a pack of lawyers stood there chatting about our case and laughing among themselves, I said, "You know, every breath they take is costing us a hundred dollars." Were they trustworthy? Did they have our best interests at heart, as they claimed? And then there was the question of how the judge would rule. In one sentence she could ruin us.

In addition to these problems with our business, we suffered in other, more personal ways. A number of our dear relatives and friends died during this time, including a beloved great-aunt who passed away in March 2003 and a cherished uncle, Bob, who succumbed to cancer in May 2004. I know it's hard to believe, but there was hardly a month that went by when we didn't have a funeral to go to or condolences to send.

And then, at the end of November 2003, what in some ways was the deepest wound of all to me, occurred. I had run home between counseling cases for a bite to eat, and I listened with shock and horror to a voicemail message from my dearest friend, Julie's, mother: "Oh, Elyse," she cried. "Richard [Julie's son] is dead. He was killed in a car accident last night." *What?* I thought. *What did I just hear?* and then, within my heart I sensed a deadly coldness that was transforming itself into rage. *Hasn't she gone through enough? Isn't this a little heavy-handed of you? I understand, Lord, why you're hammering me, but this? Why this? Isn't this over the line?*

In the days that followed, as I met with Julie and helped with the funeral arrangements and hosted the family reception at my home, questions about the ultimate goodness of God filled my heart and mind. For the first time in many years I began to question God. I questioned His character—why would He do this to her? How does this square with what He says about Himself? Is He loving? Is He merciful? I fell headlong into a pit of despair and discouragement.

What I've just written may have shocked you. I know, we Christians aren't supposed to have these questions. We're supposed to be strong and filled with faith. But this isn't the portrait that I see in the lives of brothers and sisters in Scripture, and it isn't the experience of our brothers and sisters here. This was, for me, midnight of the dark night of my soul.

The Steadfast Heart

During these difficult years the Lord graciously brought Psalm 57 to me through the preaching of one of our church's leaders, Steve Shank. Then, on my birthday at the beginning of November 2003, in kindness God gave me a present: He burned this psalm into my consciousness.

Because Phil and I were at a loss about how to pray, we had already been spending much time in the psalms. Psalm 57 was one of those psalms that spoke deeply to me. One verse in particular was meaningful. It read, "My heart is steadfast, O God, my heart is steadfast! I will sing and make melody!" (ESV). Then, for this same birthday a dear friend gave me a beautiful chain with a silver heart. Inscribed on it was my verse: "My heart is steadfast, O God." What was so remarkable about her gift was that she didn't know that God had already been speaking that verse to me. A steadfast heart? Was that God's plan for me? My heart felt anything but steadfast.

This is a book about what I've learned, and am continuing to learn, about the Lord and myself through this particular trial. God has been gracious to Phil and me during these years. He's used our suffering as the means to reveal to us new understanding about Himself, His great goodness, and our considerable need for a Savior. These lessons have been precious to us. We thank Him for them. He's used our suffering in the lives of others, as well, as they've prayed and suffered with us. We've grown to love our church and our friends more deeply than ever before.

In writing about our suffering, I want to make clear one reality: I know that what we've gone through is nothing in comparison with what others endure on a daily basis. Our trial was fashioned for us by a wise God who knew exactly what kind of suffering we needed. The trials we endure are meant to get at the idolatry, self-love, and independent unbelief that God desires to purge from our life. They're also meant to cause us to love Jesus Christ more and more, and sometimes they're not discipline at all, but rather part of God's mysterious plan to glorify himself. So, please, as you read through this book, don't compare my suffering with yours or wonder how you could endure what I've gone through or vice versa. Just recognize that God brings to each of us what will best glorify Himself.

Recently a friend shared the following poem about the gift of suffering:

The Thorn

I stood a mendicant [beggar] of God
    before His royal throne
And begged Him for a priceless gift,
    which I could call my own.
I took the gift from out His hand,
    but as I would depart,
I cried "But Lord, this is a thorn
    and it has pierced my heart.
"This is a strange, a hurtful gift
    that Thou hast given me."
He said, "My child, I give good gifts
    and give My best to thee."
I took it home and though at first,
    the cruel thorn hurt sore;
As long years passed I learned at last
    to love it more and more.
I learned He never gives a thorn
    without this added grace.
He takes the thorn to pin aside . . .
    the veil which hides His face.
           Martha Snell Nicholson

I have to admit that until this season of difficulty, I never thought of a thorn as a good gift. Please don't misunderstand what I'm saying. I could have told you about the theological purposes in suffering, but my knowledge of the blessings of suffering were mostly theoretical. *Of course God uses suffering! Of course suffering is good for us! Of course God is sovereign! Of course I need purification!* And as I have undergone the daily stab of that thorn, I am oh so thankful that God had laid this theological foundation in my heart before He placed the thorn in my hand. Or, to change metaphors, I am thankful that my heart had been protected in the lighthouse of His love even before the sky began to cloud up. But as thankful as I am that I had that solid anchorage, that sweet haven didn't completely alleviate the pain, nor could it prevent the storm from assailing us. Though the wind is still raging in some ways, I'm beginning to finally see, though dimly, His true plans for my life and how much He loves my soul. I'm learning about suffering—the suffering brought on by the fall, the suffering of a sinless Savior.

I've grown to see how self-deceived and foolish I had been before this affliction (thinking all the time that I was growing in truth and wisdom). In light of this new understanding, I've also come to understand that I'm still exceedingly deceived, foolish, proud, rebellious, and unbelieving. I don't mean to say that God hasn't accomplished His work through this, but I do mean that I've learned something of the depth of my own sinfulness that I didn't see before. I've also learned about the depth of His grace and love, and I know now, more than ever, that these are good lessons for me.

One more thought to set this book up for you: this isn't a book that's shrouded in mournful weeds of gray or black. This is a book that's glowing with luminescent embers of rekindled zeal and ardor. I'm not going to say that suffering is fun. Scripture makes it clear that suffering is "painful rather than pleasant."[1] What I do want to say, though, is that the "peaceful fruit of righteousness" that is the result of God's perfect plan for us is luscious, and there's only one way to genuinely savor this fruit: through suffering.

Since you've picked up this book, I assume that you're in the midst of a storm of some sort yourself. As we launch our little bark out onto the stormy sea together, please don't focus on the exact nature of my suffering. Although I'll refer to it, I'll do so only to illustrate a truth that I think will be helpful to you. In addition, please don't limit God's lessons for you to those I'll share here. We each have a road marked out for us by the Lord. Suffering isn't one-size-fits-all. No, He's woven the exact robe that He wants you to wear, and it will fit you perfectly, pinching where it should pinch and comforting where you need it most.

In the pages that follow we'll go topic by topic through Psalm 57. Although we will progress through the psalm in a consecutive manner, we'll also skip around a little and take some time off from the psalm to look at Jesus Christ and His experience in the storm. But we will begin with our cries for God's mercy and end where David does: "Be exalted, O God, above the heavens! Let your glory be over all the earth!" (Ps. 57:11 ESV).

At the end of every chapter, I've included a few questions for further study. Let me encourage you to plumb the depths of these questions and ask the Lord to show you what it is He is teaching you particularly. Let me also encourage you to get a journal or notebook that you're going to use as you interact with the questions.

For now, let me leave you with one passage for your contemplation:

> I know, O LORD, that your rules are righteous,
>   and that in faithfulness you have afflicted me.
> Let your steadfast love comfort me
>   according to your promise to your servant.
> Let your mercy come to me, that I may live;
>   for your law is my delight. (Ps. 119:75–77 ESV)

Our Cry in the Storm

Be merciful to me, O God, be merciful to me, for in you my
soul takes refuge; in the shadow of your wings I will take
refuge, till the storms of destruction pass by. (Ps. 57:1 ESV)

As we begin our journey together, let me encourage you
to read through Psalm 57. I've written all eleven verses
out for you below, from the English Standard Version, so that
you can copy them into your journal and interact with them.
Please resist the impulse to do what I usually do when I see
a long passage written out in a book: Please don't give it a
cursory glance. Remember, we're beginning a voyage through
a storm together, and these verses will be our guide. (If you're
not used to *interacting* with Scripture in a personal way, you
can read each verse and then ask yourself, "What purpose did
the Spirit have in writing this? What is it teaching me about

God, about myself? What would responding in faith to this teaching look like?").

> ¹Be merciful to me, O God, be merciful to me,
>> for in you my soul takes refuge;
> in the shadow of your wings I will take refuge,
>> till the storms of destruction pass by.
> ²I cry out to God Most High,
>> to God who fulfills His purpose for me.
> ³He will send from heaven and save me;
>> he will put to shame him who tramples of me.
>>> *Selah*
>
> God will send out his steadfast love and his
>> faithfulness!
>> he will put to shame him who tramples on me.
> ⁴My soul is in the midst of lions;
>> I lie down amid fiery beasts—
> the children of man, whose teeth are spears and
>> arrows,
>> whose tongues are sharp swords.
> ⁵Be exalted, O God, above the heavens!
>> Let your glory be over all the earth!
> ⁶They set a net for my steps;
>> my soul was bowed down.
> They dug a pit in my way,
>> but they have fallen into it themselves. *Selah*
> ⁷My heart is steadfast, O God,
>> my heart is steadfast!
> I will sing and make melody!
>> ⁸Awake, my glory!
> Awake, O harp and lyre!
>> I will awake the dawn!

⁹I will give thanks to you, O Lord, among the
    peoples;
  I will sing praises to you among the nations.
¹⁰For your steadfast love is great to the heavens,
    your faithfulness to the clouds.
¹¹Be exalted, O God, above the heavens!
  Let your glory be over all the earth!

Did you enjoy that experience? Did the Lord feed your heart? What did you learn about yourself, about the Lord? As I've read through this passage numbers of times I've learned some lovely lessons. For instance, from the first verse I've learned that I'm in need of mercy and that I have to depend on God to give it to me. I've also learned that God *is* kind and merciful, and even though it feels like I'm hiding in a cave, I'm hiding under the shadow of His wings. I've also learned that although storms of destruction do come upon me, they also eventually pass us by. In this superficial glance at just one verse, I've found great solace. Was it the same for you? This verse has helped me see that I'm needy and dependent, living in a world that's fallen; but He's sufficient and faithful, covering me from many of the effects of sin that I ought to have to suffer.

David's Storms of Destruction

As you and I consider David's words here, let's try to remember that this psalm wasn't written in a vacuum. It has a history, and there's a story that brings David's words to life: this background story gives the psalm color and depth. Instead of being a one-dimensional pencil sketch, it becomes a portrait brushed with rich colors and deep texture. David penned these words out of his real and grievous experiences as a man who trusted in God and yet sinned and suffered just like we do.

You'll begin to find real comfort in this passage and all the psalms when you see David's experience mirrored in your own. Have you ever been in such depth of despair and sorrow that the only prayer you could moan was, "Be merciful to me, O God. Be merciful to me"? Have you discovered in yourself such dependence and need that all you could do was plead for mercy? David knew about this kind of suffering, and the Holy Spirit inspired him to write about it so that you, here in the twenty-first century, would have hope, as Paul taught: "For whatever was written in former days was written for our instruction, that through endurance and through the encouragement of the Scriptures we might have hope" (Rom. 15:4 esv).

David's suffering had a purpose in his life, but it also has a purpose in ours. Isn't that an encouraging thought? Our suffering isn't an isolated incident that we have to muddle through. No, our suffering has a greater meaning. In the chapters to come we'll look at what some of that meaning is, but for now, let me encourage you to have hope. David cried out to God for mercy, and God answered him. You can cry out to God for mercy, and God will answer you, as well. You can rest confidently in His promised help: "Whatever you ask in My name, that will I do. . . . If you ask Me anything in My name, I will do it" (John 14:13–14). You can have hope that while the storms of destruction are raging outside, you'll be safely tucked away under the shadow of His wings.

When Samuel, the Old Testament prophet and priest, anointed young David to be the next king of Israel, perhaps David anticipated an upwardly mobile life of blessing and luxury. (If you're not familiar with David's story, you can read about it beginning at 1 Sam. 16). Indeed, events soon after this anointing would have fit with his expectations. David bravely fought Goliath and was subsequently taken into the household of King Saul. Jonathan, Saul's son, soon became David's best friend. It wasn't long until David was known by the women of Israel as a great warrior, becoming the subject of lyrics they sang: "David has killed his ten thousands." How could life get any better? Although David remained humble and loyal, looking for opportunities to bless King Saul, a change was beginning to take place. Saul's heart grew hard toward David, and Saul looked upon him with growing hatred, suspicion, and envy.

As God's predicted judgment fell on Saul, David's position in the kingdom deteriorated. Twice Saul tried to pin him to the wall with his spear. Saul banished him from his presence and sought a way to do away with him. He even offered David his daughter, Michal, for a wife as a ploy to deceitfully send him to his death. David's life was changing—and not for the better.

Although the Lord continued to prosper and bless David in some ways, Saul grew increasingly hardened by his sinful jealousy. Conflicts within the palace finally escalated to the point that Saul's son, Jonathan, advised David to flee for his life. And thus began a drawn-out and desperate season of terror, hiding, and heartache as David barely survived, existing no longer as the king's favorite but now as a hunted fugitive.

When David wrote what we refer to as Psalm 57, he was running for his life, hiding in a wilderness, in a cave. He was being pursued by a powerful king who hated him and who had marshaled three thousand warriors to hunt him down. It might have been about this time that David could have looked at his life and said, "I've been the cause of the cruel death of the priests who helped me" (1 Sam. 22); "My wife has been given to another man" (1 Sam. 25); "I have to hide my family in a foreign land" (1 Sam. 22:3); "I'm continually fleeing for my life"; and "Now, here I am hiding in this cave. How did this happen?" Humanly speaking, David's life seemed hopeless and his situation desperate. But the truth was that he was exactly where God wanted him, secreted securely in God's protecting embrace.

Sometimes we miss the truth of God's embrace and only see life the way circumstances appear on the surface. For instance, perhaps you're all too aware that your actions have unintentionally caused pain or brought calamity to someone. Perhaps you've seen relationships deteriorate, or you've watched your family endure seemingly endless suffering. Possibly you've suffered for doing good, or you're being persecuted without cause. In these and many other ways, life can almost instantaneously become something other than what we expected. Our lives frequently start out with great expectations only to be followed by long seasons of suffering and trial. Does it seem as though you're fleeing for your spiritual or physical life from an enemy? Is God really there? Is he really hiding you under the shadow of his wings?

Even though David was where God wanted him, I'm fairly certain that he didn't enjoy hiding out in a cave, running for his life. Who would? I wouldn't. Like most people, I don't like having to beg for mercy, and I'm sure you don't either. Because I still struggle with my own sin, I'd much rather have what I imagine the life of the king's pet would be, sitting on a pillow, strumming my harp in a palace as I look out through a window and survey all my kingdom. Doesn't God want me to avoid caves? He wouldn't be calling me into one, would He?

As much as I love the truth that the Lord hears my prayer, I don't like walking in the dark, and I don't like storms, humiliation, or hiding in caves from enemies. In my sinful pride, I don't like being in a position of having to beg for mercy. Frankly, I would rather ask for mercy when I feel independent and self-sufficient, foolishly assuming that God will be impressed by my humble-sounding words—just as long as I don't have to live in a cave! But I'm learning that my self-sufficient prayers for help are not what God wants from me. No, what He wants from me is a recognition of my brokenness and need. Jesus talked of this perspective in prayer. This is what He said:

> But the tax collector, standing some distance away, was even unwilling to lift up his eyes to heaven, but was beating his breast, saying, "God, be merciful to me, the sinner!" I tell you, this man went to his house justified rather than the other; for everyone who exalts himself will be humbled, but he who humbles himself will be exalted. (Luke 18:13–14)

Imagine, if you will, the humility of heart that would so permeate your self-appraisal that you can't even raise your eyes up to the Lord. Think of the soul that would afflict its own heart with a beating, in essence saying, "Thus would I smite this wicked heart of mine, the poisoned fountain out of which flow all the streams of sin, if I could come at it."[1] What was this man's prayer? "God, be merciful to me, the sinner!"

Your Trial Is the Mark of His Mercy

God is at work in your circumstance. In the same way that God was preparing David to rule his kingdom and to foreshadow the rule of the one whose kingdom will have no end, the Lord is preparing your heart to reflect the wonders of His Son. Life in the cave gives you the one good gift you really need:

a correct self-appraisal. Because of our sinful nature, without God's mercy in our lives, we all belong in caves and holes in the ground, not in fine palaces embellished with beautiful fabrics and fragrant blossoms. It's surely His mercy that we find ourselves, from time to time, in hardship and pain, discovering the great treasures of accurate self-understanding and the beauty of His merciful character. It's because we're each His favorite that we find ourselves here, now.

Life in the cave opens our eyes to our helplessness. Think about David's experience. There was no way that David could save himself. His enemies surrounded him, and he had no strength or wisdom or goodness that could change his circumstance. For a man as handsome, capable, and brave as David was, this was a needful lesson. Like all of us, he needed to see himself as unworthy of demanding anything from the Lord and in such great peril and barrenness that he didn't have anything to offer. All he could do was plead for mercy. Let's think for a moment about what it means to plead for mercy.

What does the word *mercy* mean to you? In the Bible, mercy means "compassion to one in need or helpless distress, or in debt and without claim to favourable treatment."[2] Look again at that definition:

- Compassion to one in need.
- Compassion to one in helpless distress.
- Compassion to one in debt.
- Compassion to one without claim to favorable treatment.

Do you see yourself as a person who is in need? How needy are you? We Americans prize thoughts of self-sufficiency and independence. *I did it MY way!* we vainly sing. The problem with that way of thinking, of course, is that it's an obstacle to our receiving what we desperately need (whether we know it or not): God's compassion.

Are you helpless in your distress? In the trials we've been facing, there is nothing that I can do to make things better. I'm utterly helpless. God loves to show us our helplessness because it's then that we prize His mercy. He doesn't want to build our self-confidence. He wants to build confidence in Himself; as Paul wrote, our confidence is from God (see 2 Cor. 3:5). We learn about God's strength only when we are weak and helpless.

Are you in debt? Although it's true that Phil and I were facing great financial debt, I don't think that's the debt God's primarily concerned with. He wants me to see the great debt I owe to Him: debts of obedience, love, and the ultimate debt that although I deserve His judgment, He's given me His forgiveness. In just the same way that there isn't any way that we can pay the natural debt we owe, we needed to see the great debt we owed Him that His Son paid for us. The thousands and thousands that we owed our creditors is nothing in comparison with what we owed Him, and that debt's been paid. That's mercy.

We're without claim to favorable treatment. We don't have any right to ask Him for anything except mercy. I don't deserve favorable treatment. No, I deserve the lash, the nail, the crown of thorns, the cross, and an eternity of separation from Him. When I consider my record before Him, I don't have a leg to stand on. All I can do is ask for Him not to give me what I deserve, that is, judgment, but rather to give me what I don't deserve: mercy.

It's interesting that the people that had gathered around David in his trial were described as "everyone who was in distress

. . . in debt . . . and was discontented" (1 Sam. 22:2). That's us, isn't it? We're in distress, in debt, and discontented. Those are the kinds of people God loves to gather to Himself and to pour mercy on. Mercy is such an integral part of His character that it's even one of His names. He's the Father of Mercies. Listen to how Paul describes him: "Blessed be the God and Father of our Lord Jesus Christ, the Father of mercies and God of all comfort, who comforts us in all our affliction" (2 Cor. 1:3–4). Is the Father of mercies and God of comfort comforting you?

Dark Caves, Luminous Revelations

In contradiction to our culture's beliefs, the Bible teaches us that our hearts are not formed by our circumstances or environment. Instead it teaches that our environment merely reveals what already fills our heart. This is what Jesus meant (in part) when He said that it wasn't what was outside a man that defiled him but rather what came from within him.

> For from within, out of the heart of men, proceed the evil thoughts, fornications, thefts, murders, adulteries, deeds of coveting and wickedness, as well as deceit, sensuality, envy, slander, pride and foolishness. All these evil things proceed from within and defile the man. (Mark 7:21–23)

What do the caves in our life tell us about our heart? They tell us our hearts are filled with sin and our need for a Savior is far greater than we ever knew. If I had never gone through the trials of the last four years, I would have never been aware of my love of and dependence on money, my propensity to manipulate and control, my pride and lack of love and respect for others, my endemic unbelief, and most especially my great need for Jesus.

Part of God's gracious work in my life has been to progressively reveal my sin to me. Again, it's not that I didn't know I needed Him. *It's just that I didn't know how much.* This is the bright revelation that's been illuminating the cavern that's become my home. I've come to understand how much He delights in my self-abasement. This is what Isaiah wrote:

> For thus says the high and exalted One who lives forever, whose name is Holy, "I dwell on a high and holy place, and also with the contrite and lowly of spirit in order to revive the spirit of the lowly and to revive the heart of the contrite." (Isa. 57:15)

> To this one I will look, to him who is humble and contrite of spirit, and who trembles at My word. (Isa. 66:2)

What benefits are awaiting us as God faithfully and lovingly afflicts and humbles us? These verses (and the ones from Luke 18:13–14) tell me that God's work in my life is for my good. What is the good that He's accomplishing? He's making me the sort of person He delights in. As He afflicts my heart I can see the sin that's there. And as I see that sin, I'm crushed and abased, and I recognize my need for Him. It's then that He revives, encourages, loves, comforts, changes, and fellowships with me, and my love becomes more like the love He deserves.

Think with me now about what God is doing in putting you in a cave where you have to beg for His mercy. He's drawing you ever closer to Himself by loosing you from the bonds of love that have fastened you to this earth. He's using your difficulty to open your blind eyes to your great need and dependence upon Him, and He's making His Son all the more precious to you. During the times when my life is going along swimmingly, I can stand at the foot of the cross and calmly appreciate its wonder and beauty. But when enemies whose teeth are spears and arrows, who are setting a net for my steps, surround me, I begin to understand His suffering and my great need for Him. I'm like the Israelites who, after having been bitten by fiery serpents, struggled for just one healing glance at the brazen serpent and their salvation (John 3:14–15).

When David wrote this psalm, he was probably in the cave of Adullum. As he was sitting there, in the dark both literally and figuratively, I'm sure that he didn't know what would happen in his future. He didn't have any guarantees that he'd even make it out of that cave. I can imagine that it probably seems the same way to you. It certainly did for me. Is this cave going to be my final resting place?

Although David didn't know whether he'd make it out or not, we know the end of his story. In actuality, the cave of Adullum is about two miles south of the scene of David's triumph over Saul. Think of it. The very place that seemed like it might end up being his grave was so near the place of his exaltation. He just wasn't aware of it . . . and God didn't reveal it to him. In the same way, we don't know what is around the corner for us because God isn't revealing that to us either. Why? So that we'll remain humble and contrite and close to Him.

The cave of Adullum is also only thirteen miles west of Bethlehem, where our ultimate victory and triumph was assured. In a cavern of a stall the "radiance of His glory and the exact representation of His nature" was born. In ignominy and obscurity the Son of God was brought into the world as a helpless baby. The one through whom God's mercy would flow to you and me experienced all the temptation and trial that we do (and ever so much more) and was yet without sin. He was "despised and rejected, a man of sorrows and acquainted with grief." Today you and I can beg God for mercy and rest confident that He hears us because His Son was cruelly punished for our helplessness, our debt, our discontent. Why not take time now to thank God for His mercy to you in His Son?

Finding His Comfort in the Midst of the Storm

1. Meditate on the truths of God's mercy found in the following verses: Psalms 86:5, 15; 119:76–77; Micah 7:18–19. What have you learned about God's mercy? About yourself? About your need?

2. Read the story of David and Saul from 1 Samuel 22–24. How do the trials you're facing correspond to the ones that David faced? How are they different?

3. How have you been responding to your trials? What are the good purposes of God in them? Have you been embracing them or fleeing from them?

4. Isaiah said that brokenness, contriteness, and humility of heart are precious to God. Why do you think that is?

5. Even if you see that you've consistently responded sinfully to your circumstances, please don't despair. The stripping away of any vestige of self-righteousness is one of the most precious works of God for our benefit. The Heidelberg Catechism furnishes us with a wonderful truth in answer to question 1, "What is your only comfort in life and death?" "That I, with body and soul, both in life and death, am not my own, but belong unto my faithful Savior Jesus Christ; who, with His precious blood has fully satisfied for all my sins, and delivered

me from all the power of the devil; and so preserves me that without the will of my heavenly Father not a hair can fall from my head; yea, that all things must be subservient to my salvation, wherefore by His Holy Spirit, He also assures me of eternal life, and makes me heartily willing and ready, henceforth, to live unto Him."[3]

6. Summarize what you've learned in this chapter in four or five sentences.

His Forsaken Son

We do not have a high priest who is unable to sympathize
with our weaknesses, but one who in every respect has been
tempted as we are, yet without sin. Let us then
with confidence draw near to the throne of grace,
that we may receive mercy and find grace to help
in time of need. (Heb. 4:15–16 ESV)

During the last several years, there have been many nights when I've sought out and received God's comfort. I've lain awake at 3 a.m., wondering, worrying, wishing my life was something other than it was. Then, when I finally get back to my right mind, I remember that God's comfort is near and that all I have to do is ask and I'll receive His mercy and "grace to help." *Father,* I pray, *I need your mercy, strength, and grace now. Please help me trust in you and live faithfully now. If you grant me sleep, then may I do so in peace; if you don't grant me sleep, then may I love you and glorify you. Please grant me your comfort and help me remember your truth. In Your Son's Name I pray, Amen."*

Sometimes when I pray, God helps me return to sleep. Other times He doesn't. Although I have known times when the Lord doesn't answer my prayers as I would like, there has never been a time when I've been utterly forsaken by Him. I always know that He's near and that He hears me simply because He's promised to be there. These are His promises to you and me:

> Do not fear, for I am with you; do not anxiously look about you, for I am your God. I will strengthen you, surely I will help you, surely I will uphold you with My righteous right hand. (Isa. 41:10)

> The afflicted and needy are seeking water, but there is none, and their tongue is parched with thirst; I, the LORD, will answer them Myself, as the God of Israel I will not forsake them. (Isa. 41:17)

> I will ask the Father, and He will give you another Helper, that He may be with you forever; that is the Spirit of truth . . . He abides with you and will be in you. I will not leave you as orphans; I will come to you. (John 14:16–18)

> I am with you always, even to the end of the age. (Matt. 28:20)

> He Himself has said, "I will never desert you, nor will I ever forsake you." (Heb. 13:5–6)

> For the LORD will not abandon His people, nor will He forsake His inheritance. (Ps. 94:14)

Even though I do not deserve this kindness, in His mercy God has promised to be with me. He won't forsake us because He's pledged Himself to be with us in all our trials. This is an astonishing truth, isn't it?

In this chapter, we're going to deviate from our progression through Psalm 57 to look more deeply into the life of the Son. It's appropriate to do so because Psalm 57, although written by David and for our edification, is primarily a psalm about the sufferings of Jesus Christ.[1] Why not take a moment to read Psalm 57 again, this time as though it were a prayer of your Lord?

The Accursed Cup

There is marvelous and enduring comfort in the knowledge that God's presence abides with us. But there is a truth that's even more astonishing. Think about this: The only begotten Son of God cried out in anguish, "My God, My God, why have you forsaken me?" (Matt. 27:46 ESV).

From all eternity—a distance in time unfathomable for us to comprehend—the Father and the Son were one. The Lord plainly said, "I and the Father are one" (John 10:30), and His original hearers knew exactly what He meant: He claimed to be fully divine. He was God. He wasn't merely one in purpose or power, He was God. He and His Father were one.

How is it then that He who was one with God might be forsaken by Him? As Luther asked, "God forsaken by God! Who can understand it?"[2] Drink deeply of this precious sovereign remedy, dear sister, and let it speak honeyed volumes of assurance and confidence into your tormented soul: He cried out so that you wouldn't have to! He was forsaken so that you wouldn't be!

In the depths of suffering into which He had then sunk . . . horrible and death-like terror appalled Him, and such infernal temptations roared around Him, that a feeling came over Him, as if He were exiled from the fellowship of God, and entirely given up to the infernal powers. Not only did all the horrors which were produced in the world from the dreadful womb of sin expand themselves before Him, but He also entered, with His holy soul, in a manner incomprehensible to us, into the fellowship of our consciousness of guilt, and emptied the whole of the horrible cup of the wages of sin. . . .[3]

For you and me, the Lord "tasted the bitterest drop in the accursed cup . . . being forsaken of God." Although you may truly feel misery and affliction, you've not felt this. You've never been forsaken by God. You've never enjoyed the fellowship Jesus had with His Father, a fellowship so sweet that the loss of it would rend your heart. You've not tasted the bitterest drop in the cup of God's wrath—and because He groaned in forsaken agony, you never will.

I know that there have been times in my life when I felt that I had been forsaken. When I felt that no one was there with me, when I was walking through the valley of the shadow of death, isolated and alone. But I've never felt what He felt. His agonized cry is meant to dry our tears, as we consider that our suffering is but for a "moment," (2 Cor. 4:17), and we'll never have to cry out, "Why have I been forsaken?" as we rejoice in a land of endless day and wonderful happiness.

In our trials, it's important for us to remember that everything we have was purchased for us by a merciful and loving Savior. He was forsaken so that we would not be. He was punished so that we could be set free. The assurance that we have in the midst of our storm is that God's ear is always open to our cry and that He's not punishing us for our sins but rather has poured out every drop of His just wrath on His innocent Son.

Yes, we are suffering, but our suffering is not judgment for our sin, will not be eternal, and is something we don't walk through alone. It is true that there are times when we reap the consequences of our sin, but even in this reaping, we're not being punished by God. He does discipline us, but His discipline is always redemptive and remedial, never punitive. He does correct us for our good and out of love, but if we're in His Son, we'll never know His eternal judgment and displeasure. He's with us even in our failures and is using them to benefit our soul and cause us to love the cross more and more.

Now that you've had a moment to contemplate the marvelous suffering of your Savior, let's revisit the verses we looked at before but this time with a more personal twist:

You need not fear or anxiously look around for help: He is your God. The one who endured the worst of it for you will strengthen, help and uphold you! (Isa. 41:10)

Even though you feel afflicted, needy, and dry, I, the one who called out, "I thirst" for your sake will come to you myself; I will water and comfort you; you won't be forsaken! (Isa. 41:17)

Because He loves you, and because He is so kind, He promises never to leave you alone. You aren't an orphan, searching through the world for a Father who will love, protect, and provide for you. Even though you don't see His physical body, He has given you His Spirit to comfort you, and He'll give you all the assurance and truth that you need. (John 14:16–18)

43

Even though it seems like days and days have passed with no change in your circumstances or the troubles of the world, He's promising that He'll be with you forever—even to the end of time. Let the cross remind you how much He loves you and how true He is to His word—He is with you even now. (Matt. 28:20)

You can trust Him not to desert you in fear or weakness, because He's already been through the worst of it and come out victorious! (Heb.13:5–6)

Even though you may have been abandoned by family or friends, He will never abandon you. You are His inheritance—you are His reward! (Ps. 94:14)

Fixing Your Eyes on Him

The writer to the Hebrews, a group of people suffering terribly for their faith, wrote,

> Therefore, since we have so great a cloud of witnesses surrounding us, let us also lay aside every encumbrance and the sin which so easily entangles us, and let us run with endurance the race that is set before us, fixing our eyes on Jesus, the author and perfecter of faith, who for the joy set before Him endured the cross, despising the shame, and has sat down at the right hand of the throne of God. For consider Him who has endured such hostility by sinners against Himself, so that you will not grow weary and lose heart. (Heb. 12:1–3)

How can we find the strength that we need to endure? How can we avoid weary heartlessness? The writer to the Hebrews gives us the answer. We're to fix our eyes on Him. I know that it would be easy to overlook the importance of this counsel, so let's take a closer look.

The Greek word *aphorao,* translated "fixing" in this version, means to "look away from one thing to . . . see another."[4] As we endure suffering, whether it's the suffering of our sin, the suffering of someone else's sin against us, or the suffering that's endemic in a fallen world, we're to transfer the focus of our eyes from our suffering to His. We're to "concentrate our gaze"[5] upon Him. We're to shift our sight off our pain, and we're to consider how He suffered and why.

He suffered as the author and finisher of your faith. The reason that you and I even have faith today and the reason you can be assured you'll have faith through all your tomorrows is His suffering. Because He suffered in the crucible of God's perfect will: that He should be born as a man, suffer under wicked authorities, and die for our sin, He's now known as the Man of Sorrows. And because He did so in faith from beginning to end, you can be assured that your faith, no matter what cup you're called to drink, will not fail. Your faith can't fail because His didn't.[6]

Because He "looked away" from His sufferings to the "joy that was set before Him," you can rest peacefully in the truth that joy is assured to you, too. As you set your gaze on the one who fixed His eyes resolutely on the joy of pleasing His Father, you'll find that same pleasure filling your heart. Today, in the midst of your suffering and pain, you're pleasing to the Father because He was. You can know the joy of unbounded peace with God because Jesus' joy was centered on your ultimate reconciliation and delight.

What did He endure for you? He endured the shame of bearing a curse and being a curse for us. Galatians 3:13 cites the

Law in stating that everyone who is hanged on a tree is cursed, detestable, or abhorred. Not only was He cursed as a law breaker and executed on a tree for capital crimes, but He also became a curse itself for our sake. In becoming a curse for us He voluntarily underwent the penalty for a life of lawlessness. What was the curse? What is the greatest curse any created being can know? To be cut off from God—to be forsaken by Him.

He became a curse so that we law breakers might receive the blessing promised to law keepers (Deut. 28–29). This blessing is the ultimate fulfillment of the blessing promised to Abraham: "And in you all the families of the earth will be blessed" (Gen. 12:3) and "I will be [your] God" (Gen. 17:8). He is Immanuel, the holy God who resides with sinful man, and His residence with us is the blessing that was promised thousands of years ago. It is the blessing that was lost in the garden and is restored on a desolate hill. Fix the eyes of your heart on this truth: He became a curse and was cut off as a law breaker so that you would be a blessing and know the blessing of unhindered communion with Him.

The passage in Hebrews continues on to say that He "despised" the shame that was part and parcel with the curse and being hung on a cross. This word *despised* is interesting. It means to think slightly of someone or something. Did He think about the shame? Yes, He did. But He didn't fix His attention on it. His attention was otherwise occupied with something more important: with you and the joy He would know as you were blessed in Him. He knew that great blessing and joy would come to Him—after all, He is the one who said, "It is more blessed to give than to receive" (Acts 20:35). That's just what He did, wasn't it? He gave so that we could receive!

Where is He now? He's sitting at the right hand of the throne of God in heaven. No longer forsaken or abandoned, He's there at the position of authority in the presence of His Father. And what is He doing? He's displaying His scars. Although everyone else in heaven will have new, resurrection bodies, without weakness or scar, He will still bear His. He displays His scars so that whenever your enemy comes into the throne room of heaven to accuse you of sin (Rev. 12:10) before the Father, your Savior stands and displays the marks of His suffering. "Father," He declares, "that debt has already been paid!" And because He's there, in His Father's presence, you can fix your attention on your future home. You'll join the one who loves you unimaginably, and you'll spend eternity gazing at His wounds and thanking Him for His faithful suffering.

Does His suffering matter to you today? Yes, of course it does. Because of His suffering you can know that your suffering won't last. And that the greatest suffering, that of being rightly accused of sin and being found guilty, has no possibility of ever falling on you. You'll never be cursed as a law breaker! And because of His suffering, the afflictions you're enduring now will certainly come to an end.

How are we to respond to this? How are our hearts to be affected? We're to consider the way sinners (like us) treated Him, and we're to persevere in faith. If He did that for me, a sinner, then I can persevere in this distress for Him. And I know that I will endure because it doesn't depend on my strength but on the strength He's already purchased for me.

Adam Clarke, a godly man who lived in the 1700s, wrote of this passage in Hebrews,

Attentively observe and analyze every part of [Christ's] conduct, enter into his spirit, examine his motives and [purpose], and remember that, as he acted, ye are called to act; he will furnish you with the same Spirit, and will support you with the same strength. He bore a continual opposition of sinners against himself; but he conquered by meekness, patience, and perseverance: he has left you an example that ye should follow his steps. If ye trust in him, ye shall receive strength; therefore, howsoever great your opposition may be, ye shall not be weary: if ye confide in and attentively look to him, ye shall have continual courage to go on, and never faint in your minds.[7]

You're Following in His Steps

Around A.D. 65, Peter wrote a letter to suffering Christians who had been exiled because of their faith. In this letter he talked frequently about the sufferings of Christ and the part they are to play in the lives of those who are endeavoring to follow Him.

In 1 Peter 2:21, this is what he said: "You have been called for this purpose, since Christ also suffered for you, leaving you an example for you to follow in His steps." If you didn't read that last verse carefully, let me encourage you to go back and do so. It lucidly declares God's plan for your life. What is God's call, our purpose? To suffer as He did! Into our self-protected, insulated, comfortable lives, God speaks words antithetical to our self-centered philosophies and desires. His calling on your life is that you would follow in His steps.

A while ago, Christians in America were taken up with the anagram WWJD or What Would Jesus Do? Although the thought of Christ-centered obedience is proper, the real question we should ask instead is WDJD, or What *Did* Jesus Do? The answer? He suffered. It's only in His suffering that we can find how we're to live; it's only because of His suffering that we find ourselves able to follow after Him.

Let's face it. That's not the picture of Christianity we're usually exposed to. We've been taught to think that being a Christian means the end of all our troubles and having all our perceived needs met. I think that's one reason why we all struggle so much in trials: we're expecting something else. Peter counsels us in this also,

> Beloved, do not be surprised at the fiery trial when it comes upon you to test you, as though something strange were happening to you. But rejoice insofar as you share Christ's sufferings, that you may also rejoice and be glad when his glory is revealed. (1 Peter 4:12–13 esv)

We tend to react so strongly against storms in our lives because we are expecting something else: we're expecting heaven now. But we haven't been promised heaven yet. What we have been promised is the privilege of walking in His footsteps— footsteps that brought blessing and comfort, footsteps that walked through a garden and up a hill into death. Thankfully, for us, the sting of this life has been removed because we won't ever be abandoned to walk alone.

What is the Lord doing in your trials? He's teaching you the joys of the basin and the towel (John 13:5); of nights spent in wrestling against sin; or bearing with the weaknesses of others for the sake of the kingdom. We're learning to walk like He did.

Psalm 57 begins with two cries for mercy. "Be merciful to me, O God, be merciful to me, for in you my soul takes refuge; in the shadow of your wings I will take refuge till the storms of destruction pass by" (Ps. 57:1 ESV). Because Jesus suffered, you can pray this prayer today. Because He was refused refuge when storms of destruction raged about Him, you can hide yourself under the shadow of God's wings—safe and secure while the pernicious holocaust rages on. His soul wasn't protected as Daniel's was—He was "in the midst of lions, [He] lay down amid fiery beasts, the children of man, whose teeth are spears and arrows, whose tongues are sharp swords. They set a net for [His] steps, His soul was bowed down, they dug a pit in His way (Ps. 57:4, 6 paraphrased).

Does His suffering matter to you today? Yes, in every way. Because He suffered the crushing of God, because His soul was grieved and afflicted, today you can pray, "God be merciful to me," and you can know you'll be heard.

Perhaps the Lord isn't answering your prayer for deliverance today. Perhaps He will answer it in the future or in some way that will utterly astound you. We don't know what tomorrow will hold, but we do know one thing: we can cry to Him for mercy and have confident assurance that He hears us and hides us from the worst of the storm. Sometimes we're frightened by the howling of the wind or the pelting of the hail upon the windows of our soul, but we're never left alone in the storm, trying to find our way to some, any, safe harbor. We're neatly tucked away under the wings of our Father, who turned His back on His perfect Son so that He could turn completely toward us.

God, be merciful to me, you can pray, and you can know that He hears you because His Son was

> despised and forsaken of men, a man of sorrows and ac-
> quainted with grief; and like one from whom men hide their
> face He was despised, and we did not esteem Him. Surely
> our griefs He Himself bore, and our sorrows He carried; yet

we ourselves esteemed Him stricken, smitten of God, and afflicted. But He was pierced through for our transgressions, He was crushed for our iniquities; the chastening for our well-being fell upon Him, and by His scourging we are healed. He was oppressed and He was afflicted. . . .(Isa. 53:3–5, 7)

The Real Passion of the Christ

Is your soul being watered as you contemplate the love of our Savior? I pray that it is. Let me pour another cup of grace for you now from the writing of the prophet Isaiah. In Isaiah 53, our Lord of glory is described as a man of sorrows. Think of that. The glorious and eternal second person of the Holy Trinity is called a man of sorrows.

Hymn writer Philip P. Bliss sought to capture the wonderful juxtaposition of these two titles when he penned the words, "Man of Sorrows, what a name for the Son of God who came." What a name indeed! There is no other religion that would dare take such a name for its God. Think on this: a God who is also a man of sorrows. All other religions have gods who are powerful and who wouldn't ever suffer—especially not for the sins of others. That our "spotless Lamb of God" would not only allow Himself to be called this name but would embrace it as His own that He might reclaim ruined, guilty, and vile sinners is astounding.

As I've gone through this (and many other) times of suffering, I know that I've tended to be more impressed with my suffering than I am with His. Is His suffering more important to you than your present circumstance?

I know that your suffering probably seems more personal, more in-your-face, more tangible to you. *Yes,* you might be thinking, *He suffered . . . and I do appreciate it. But how does that help me today in my suffering?* This is the place where faith can speak into your circumstance and give you a godly perspective. As you contemplate what you've read here, pray that the Lord will open your heart to receive the great comfort that is to come to you as you ponder His afflictions.

Finding His Comfort in the Midst of Your Storm

1. Read all of Isaiah 53 and list the words that describe how the Lord suffered for you.

2. How does His suffering speak to your heart of God's vast and sacrificial love for you? Paul reminded the Romans, "He who did not spare His own Son, but delivered Him over for us all, how will He not also with Him freely give us all things?" (Rom. 8:32). God will not allow you to suffer one moment longer than is absolutely necessary for you to know the joy of being like Him. Do you trust in His love?

3. First Peter 2:22–25 tells us about the suffering of the Son for us. What parts of this passage are particularly meaningful to you? Why?

4. Perhaps thinking about Christ's suffering in this way is new for you. Why not spend a few moments asking that He make His passion more meaningful to you than it has ever been? Allow Him to pour the balm of His love into your soul as you face your troubles.

5. Summarize what you've learned in this chapter in four or five sentences.

His Suffering Saints

*They were stoned, they were sawn in two, they were
tempted, they were put to death with the sword; they went
about in sheepskins, in goatskins, being destitute, afflicted,
ill-treated (men of whom the world was not worthy),
wandering in deserts and mountains and caves and holes
in the ground. (Heb. 11:37–38)*

I'm sure you've received the same advertising brochures
from Christian book stores that I have. You know the ones
I mean. They have glossy pictures of books that will help you
"go higher, rise above obstacles, and live in health, abundance,
and victory."[1]

In contrast, in this chapter you'll learn about brothers and
sisters who were abased, felt crushed under burdens of affliction, lived with illness and deprivation, and trusted solely in

the victory of Christ on a barbarous cross. The history of some of these people is found in Scripture:

> They were stoned, they were sawn in two, they were tempted, they were put to death with the sword; they went about in sheepskins, in goatskins, being destitute, afflicted, ill-treated (men of whom the world was not worthy), wandering in deserts and mountains and caves and holes in the ground. (Heb. 11:37–38)

These faithful saints have names like Enoch, Noah, Abraham, Joseph, and Moses. They were shut up with animals on an ark for a year; wandered in the desert far from home; were sold as slaves, falsely accused; were mistreated and ultimately disappointed by their own sin. They're remembered in narratives in the Old and New Testaments. Their failures and successes are plainly told in trustworthy stories that are meant to give you and me a matter-of-fact perspective on our lives. These saints didn't always live in health, abundance, and victory. In fact, many of them eschewed wealth and comfort to follow the Lord. Others suffered martyrdom and imprisonment, exile and isolation. This is the true picture of the life of the man or woman of faith. This is what we should expect.

Please don't misunderstand what I'm saying. I'm not saying that we shouldn't expect our lives to be filled with joy and blessing or that God isn't gracious to us in giving us many good things to enjoy. He is kind and has blessed us with abundant temporal and eternal blessings. But we mustn't assume that God's goal in our lives is to make us healthy, prosperous, and victorious in every circumstance. This modern perspective would make sense only in a context where one had all (or even more than all) one wanted and suffered from a severely myopic faith characterized by the belief that God is in relationship with mankind because He is lonely and in need of love. This lie gives way to the belief that He's our cosmic therapist, dispensing spiritual mood altering drugs and platitudes focused on self-actualization and self-aggrandizement all in the name of faith and healthy thinking.

The Bible's perspective is that there is something more than this earth and the joys to be found here. There's real joy to be had and a real faith that goes on even when our sight tells us that it's no use.

Pop Beads and Pearls

When I was in elementary school, I used to play with pop beads. Did I just date myself? Oh, well. For those of you who aren't quite my age, let me tell you about pop beads. Pop beads are . . . yes, well, beads that go "pop" when you pull them apart. They're made of plastic and have a little connecting piece with a ball on the end that you can force into a hole in another bead to make a necklace or bracelet for you or a friend. Then, when you're tired of the look of it, you can pull the whole thing apart, pop, pop, pop, and start all over again. Pop beads are fun. Pop, pop, pop.

But, if you were so inclined (and endowed), you could purchase high-quality cultured Japanese pearls for upward of $40,000 for a sixteen-inch strand. These pearls would be the best in the world in what matters for pearls: color, shape, luster, quality, and origin. I've learned that pearls that are the most valued come from Akoya oysters in Japan. So, if you had a strand of Akoya pearls, you wouldn't pull it apart. No pop, pop, pop here. Just "wow."

Now, let me ask you, what would you rather have, pop beads or Akoya pearls? If I were going to give you one strand of either one, which would you choose? That's sort of a no-brainer, isn't it? Pop beads are fun, but Akoya pearls are valuable. Fun is temporary, but value lasts.

Here's the point: What God is doing in you might not be as fun as an afternoon with your pals exchanging beads and fashioning new jewelry for each other. Since you're reading this book, I'm assuming you're not living through a time of fun. What God is doing in you isn't fun, but it's precious, it's eternal, it's to be cherished. He's creating within you a faith that's worth more a world full of Akoya pearls.

I'm sure you know how pearls are formed, but just to remind you, let me briefly outline the process. The oyster is a mollusk that lives inside a shell. As the oyster grows, so does its shell, as the oyster adds layer upon layer to it. Simply put, the pearl is formed in the same way as the inside of the shell—layer upon layer, but unlike the inside of the shell, these layers are laid over an irritant, such as a grain of sand, that's gotten between the oyster and the inside of the shell. Pearls are the way that God created the oyster to protect itself from foreign substances. In sum, pearls are the consequence of an irritation.

In contradiction to most of what we read about in so-called Christian self-help books, we don't get the result of a pearl-like faith without the process of pearl making. What you're experiencing is this precious process, a process that James spoke of to his suffering readers:

> Count it all joy, my brothers, when you meet trials of various kinds, for you know that the testing of your faith produces steadfastness. And let steadfastness have its full effect, that

you may be perfect and complete, lacking in nothing. (James 1:2–4 esv)

If you're like me, you want a faith that is mature, complete, and whole. We sincerely desire a faith that brings glory to our Father, a faith that stands strong in the storm, a faith that speaks about the great treasure in knowing and loving God. But that faith can't be purchased from your local toy store. That kind of faith grows only in the environment of trial. That's what James is saying to us. Trials, in themselves, are not joyous; they're joyous only because they're effective. God in His kindness knows exactly how much sand to slip into the shell of your heart. Perhaps that sand will take the form of other people, like it did in David's life (Ps. 57:3–4, 6). Or perhaps it will come to you as deprivation, illness, or loss. He knows the exact composition of the sand you need, and He knows how long it will take to form that one great pearl both of you are looking for. Because we'll talk more about this verse in subsequent chapters, I'll leave you with this thought: He's testing your faith, and that testing will produce a steadfastness and will cause your faith to be mature, complete, and whole.

Dorothy L. Sayers, a contemporary of C. S. Lewis, has this perspective on the suffering of the Christian:

[Christianity] is the *only* religion which gives value to evil and suffering. It affirms—not, like Christian Science, that evil has no real existence, nor like Buddhism, that good consists in a refusal to experience evil—but that perfection is attained through the active and positive effort to wrench a real good out of a real evil.[2]

The Lord is using your affliction in the same way that He used affliction in the lives of millions of believers before you. He's teaching you to have faith to believe that real good can come out of the real evil that is plaguing you. He's not primarily interested in loading you up with pop beads, nor will He burden you down with more sand than is absolutely necessary. He's causing you to make real pearls, jewelry fit for a woman betrothed to a King.

Saints Who Grew in Faith

Let's take a brief excursion through the primary chapter on people of faith in Scripture, Hebrews 11. Remember that Hebrews is written to believing Jews who were suffering profoundly for their faith, and Hebrews 11 in particular is written to remind them of the faith of the saints who went before them.

The chapter begins with Abel, who "offered to God a more acceptable sacrifice than Cain" (Heb. 11:4 ESV), was commended for it, and then murdered by his brother. The text then proceeds to Enoch, who had this testimony: he pleased God so much that the Lord took him to Himself without Enoch having to die. We all know the story of Noah, whom God saved from destruction. Jeremiah Burroughs, an English Puritan who wrote in the seventeenth century, said,

> You know how Noah was put into the Ark, with all kinds of creatures shut up with him for twelve months together—it was a mighty thing, yet God having shut him up, even though the waters were assuaged, Noah was not to come out of the Ark till God bid him.[3]

Have you ever considered what Noah's life must have been like for those twelve months? I'm sure that he longed to be freed from the prison that was also his salvation, but he had to wait until God had completed the work He was committed to accomplish in him and in the world.

Consider with me now the journeys of Abraham. He was graciously chosen by God to be the father of our faith (see Rom. 4:16), and he left his home without knowing where he was going. He looked forward to the fulfillment of God's promises to him and his wife, but he was afflicted for many years as he awaited God's provision. He was sorely tested when God asked him to offer up Isaac. Have you thought about how great his affliction was as he journeyed to Mount Moriah to kill the promised son he'd waited years for?

Sarah, too, suffered the devastating affects of infertility, in unbelief resorted to fleshly measures to try to fulfill the promise on her own, and then had to live with the consequences of her unbelief. Each of these saints "died in faith, not having received the things promised," but they acknowledged that they were "strangers and exiles on the earth" (Heb. 11:13 ESV). Have you thought deeply about those words, "strangers and exiles on the earth"? Doesn't much of the trouble we have with our troubles stem from the concept that this world is our home and it ought to be a nice place to live? How do exiles in foreign countries live, I wonder?

The chapter goes on to speak of Moses, who chose rather to be "mistreated with the people of God than to enjoy the fleeting pleasures of sin. He considered the reproach of Christ greater wealth than the treasures of Egypt" (Heb. 11:25–26 ESV). We could say that Moses wanted pearls instead of pop beads, couldn't we?

What about the suffering of Joseph? Think for a moment about the afflictions he faced: he was despised by his brothers and thrown into a pit to be kept for execution. Only the righteousness of one brother, Reuben, saved him from death, but he was sentenced to a life of slavery. He was wrenched away from his father and brother Benjamin and sent to be a slave in Egypt. While there he was falsely accused and sent to prison. Then, in prison, he helped Pharoah's officials, and when he might have had hope that they would help him, the Bible says, "Yet the chief cupbearer did not remember Joseph, but forgot him" (Gen. 40:23 ESV). Psalm 105:17–19 gives us a clear picture of his trials: "Joseph . . . was sold as a slave. They afflicted his feet with fetters, He himself was laid in irons; Until the time that his word came to pass, the word of the LORD tested him."

What about the suffering of Rahab the prostitute or "Gideon, Barak, Samson, Jephthah . . . David and Samuel," who

> through faith conquered kingdoms, enforced justice, obtained promises [sounds pretty exciting so far!], stopped the mouths of lions, quenched the power of fire, escaped the edge of the sword, were made strong out of weakness [that doesn't sound so great!]. . . . Others suffered mocking and flogging, and even chains and imprisonment. They were stoned, they were sawn in two, they were killed with the sword. They went about in skins of sheep and goats, destitute, afflicted and mistreated." (Heb. 11:33–34, 36–37 ESV)

This is the testimony of the saints who have been commended for their faith, weak though it was. They didn't know anything about a Christianity that promised "health, abundance, and victory." They knew that this world was fallen and that it wasn't their home.

People of Whom the World Is Not Worthy

Let's think now about the suffering of others who are remembered for their faith . . . and the way they suffered.

Lady Jane Kenmure, a Scottish woman born in 1600, was no stranger to grief. A devout woman, she was married to a man who succumbed to the lure of worldly advancement and had become careless and profane. Early in 1629, she suffered the loss of her first daughter, followed by the death of a second and third in 1633 and 1634. Then, in the autumn of 1634, she also lost her husband, shortly after he had finally embraced Christ and turned from his worldliness. "Just a month or two after the death of her husband, she gave birth to a son and it is not hard to imagine that all her devotion was heaped upon the child."[4] Then, almost inconceivably, in 1639, her beloved son, John, died at the age of four, and she was bereft. Samuel Rutherford, her pastor, wrote to her,

> Subscribe to the Almighty's will; put your hand to the pen, and let the cross of your Lord Jesus have your submissive and resolute AMEN. . . . I shall believe, for my part, that He mindeth to distill heaven out of this loss . . . for wisdom devised it, and love laid it on, and Christ owneth it as His own, and putteth your shoulder beneath only a piece of it. . . ."[5]

* * *

In 1895, a young, godly woman, Amy Carmichael, was commissioned by the Church of England Zenana Missionary Society to go to Dohnavur, India, where she served fifty-six years as God's devoted servant—all without a furlough. A major part of her work there was devoted to rescuing children who had been dedicated by their families to be temple prostitutes. As Amy worked with the destitute Indians, she realized God had given her a love for those that the world deemed unlovely. God used the overflow of this love to start the Dohnavur Fellowship, which became a place of safety and refuge for temple children. More than a thousand children were rescued from neglect and abuse during Amy's lifetime. To them she was known as Amma, which means "mother" in the Tamil language. The world in which she lived and worked was often dangerous and stressful. Yet she never forgot God's promise to "keep her in all things." Amy spoke of dark days "when the sky turned black for me because of what I heard and knew was true . . . Sometimes it was as if I saw the Lord Jesus Christ kneeling alone, as He knelt long ago under the olive trees . . . And the only thing that one who cared could do, was to go softly and kneel down beside Him, so that He would not be alone in His sorrow over the little children."[6]

Because Amy Carmichael's life was one of Christ-centered suffering, she was able to write,

> Hast thou no scar?
> No hidden scar on foot, or side, or hand?
> I hear thee sung as mighty in the land,
> I hear them hail thy bright ascendant star,
> Hast thou no scar?
> Hast thou no wound?
> Yet I was wounded by the archers, spent,
> Leaned Me against a tree to die; and rent
> By ravening beasts that compassed Me, I swooned:
> Hast thou no wound?

No wound, no scar?
Yet, as the Master shall the servant be,
And, pierced are the feet that follow Me;
But thine are whole: can he have followed far
Who has no wounds nor scar?[6]

* * *

In 1967, Joni Eareckson Tada was confined to a wheelchair after a diving accident. The great suffering that she has endured for nearly four decades as a quadriplegic speaks of Christ's ability to "ordain what He hates to accomplish what He loves."[7] Joni's life speaks volumes to millions of people who have been afflicted with every kind of physical ailment. Joni has learned about the Savior's ability to embrace each of us in our affliction and to give us Himself. She writes,

> In Psalm 18 He is our Rock and Deliverer. In Psalm 10 He becomes the Father to the orphaned. In Isaiah 9 He is the Wonderful Counselor to the confused and depressed. If you are the one at the center of the universe, holding it together so it doesn't split apart at the seams, if everything moves, breathes, and has its being in you, as it says of God in Acts 17:28, you can do no more than give yourself. . . God doesn't give those who hurt mere words. He gives the Word—Jesus, the bruised and bloody Man of Sorrows who endured hell on earth so that you and I, by trusting in Him, can escape it.[8]

* * *

Pastor Richard Wurmbrand spent years in prison for preaching the gospel during the 1940s and 1950s in Communist-dominated Romania. He spent three years in solitary confinement and endured endless days of deprivation and torture. In testimony to the United States Senate, he recalled his imprisonment and torture:

> There were different cells. In solitary confinement I was nearly 3 years. It was in the most beautiful building of Bucharest . . . And 10 meters beneath the earth are the cells. There are no windows in the cells. Air enters through a tube. And there were a few desks with a mattress, with a straw mattress. You had but three steps for to walk. Never were we taken out from these cells except for interrogations when prisoners were beaten and tortured. For years I have never seen sun, moon, flowers, snow, stars, no man except the interrogator who beat [me], but I can say I have seen heaven open, I have seen Jesus Christ, I have seen the angels and we were very happy there. But the treatment was very bad. The purpose was to make us mad. You didn't hear a noise. A whisper you didn't hear in this cell. The guard had felt shoes. For years, not to hear anything. In all these years of prison we never had a book, we never had a bit of paper, we never had a newspaper, nothing to distract our mind. . . . Never will a Westerner understand, if I would not have the mark on my body, which are my credentials.[9]

In 1991, Richard Wurmbrand went quietly into heaven, to finally find, after years of pain inflicted by his torturers, solace and relief. We also know that he found joy and comfort in His Savior's words, "Well done, good and faithful servant." What a reunion that must have been!

The Suffering Saints and You

One time I heard someone quote a Christian from Africa who said, "When you Christians in America have a heavy burden, you pray that the Lord will transfer it off your backs. When we Christians in Africa have a heavy burden, we pray that the Lord will make our backs stronger."

It's obvious, isn't it, that we live in a time and a context that preaches comfort, wealth, and self-focused success? In God's kind providence, He doesn't call many of us to live the kind of lives that Lady Jane Kenmure or Amy Carmichael lived. He puts on us only what we can bear, and He leaves it there only as long as is absolutely necessary. We're so prosperous, we're so blessed. But as we fight to hang on to all this prosperity and blessing, we're fighting against God's good plan in our lives. He wants to adorn our souls with pearls, and we tend to want to settle for pop beads.

Paul's encouragement to his beloved Corinthian Christians as they faced affliction and trial was to "be steadfast, immovable, always abounding in the work of the Lord, knowing that your toil is not in vain in the Lord" (1 Cor. 15:58).

Do you believe that the toil God is calling you to is not "in vain"? As you join with all the other suffering saints who have ever lived, you can pray that God would make your back stronger, that He would grant you the grace to be steadfast, immovable, and always overflowing in your work for the Lord. How can you do this? By remembering that although your faith in this storm might seem meaningless, it's not! What we do for Him, how we suffer in faith, is never senseless. It always has a purpose—even though you and I might not know what that purpose is right then. You can also remember that this affliction, which seems to draw your attention to it so frequently, is a pearl in the making. Why not take time now to work through the questions below and ask Him to give you His perspective on the suffering of His saints?

Finding His Comfort in the Midst of Your Storm

1. What do you believe about God's use of suffering in your life? In the lives of His people? Do you believe that being a Christian guarantees a trouble-free, easy life? Have you heard that kind of teaching before?

2. Read Hebrews 11 and list all the people who are displayed as having faith. What kind of life did they live? How does that perspective line up with the perspective of modern American Christianity?

3. A Christian poet, Faith Cook, has taken some of the letters of Puritan pastor Samuel Rutherford and put them into verse. Below is one she wrote distilling the thoughts of Rutherford after the death of Lady Jane Kenmure's fourth child, the son she loved.

Christ Shares His People's Sorrows

O child of God this grief
That bows your spirit low
Is yours but half, for Christ Himself,
Still shares His people's woe.

His wisdom planned it out
Then bore it on His heart
Till gently on your untried back
Love laid the lesser part.

So take it all with joy,
Together bear the cross,
For while you suffer He distills,
A heaven from your loss.

Beneath His secret will
Subscribe with ready pen,
Add to this sorrow God has sent
A resolute "Amen."

Each day spend out in faith,
Nor prove His labor vain;
Cast still on Christ the pressing weight
Who only can sustain.

To Lady Kenmure
On the death of her son
October 1639
Letter 287[10]

Respond to those words with thoughts of your own.

4. Summarize what you've learned in this chapter in four
   or five sentences.

—— 4 ——

He Comforts His Children

In the shadow of your wings I will take refuge, till the storms
of destruction pass by. (Ps. 57:2 ESV)

During the summer of 2005, National Geographic released a fascinating documentary about the life cycle of Antarctic birds entitled *The March of the Penguins.* This wonderful movie, a surprise summer hit, told the story of emperor penguins, who live in one of the harshest environments on earth, and their struggle to reproduce.

The movie documents their sixty-mile trek and intricate mating ritual, after which the female lays one egg, which the male then has to balance precariously on top of his feet, under his downy coat for weeks, while the mother returns to the ocean to feed and regain strength. During the severe winter months, thousands of fathers huddle together trying to sustain their own lives and going weeks without food. If, by some accident, the egg slips off the father's feet, it will freeze almost immediately on the ice. If the egg is incubated properly, and if the chick hatches, both the male and the female will take turns protecting the tiny life from the cruel winter winds. Again, if the young chick wanders away from the warmth and protection of its parent, it will freeze to death almost immediately. This portrait of parental sacrifice and the dependence and frailty of the young is remarkable.

The March of the Penguins, while inducing wonder and worship in my heart at the wisdom of the Creator, serves also as a lovely picture of our relationship with our heavenly Father. The Bible teaches us that He tucks us carefully and lovingly under His wings to protect us from the storms of destruction that pass us by. Like baby penguins, we're so frail that the storms that assail us would destroy us if we didn't have His steadfast love and sustaining grace. David wrote, "In you my soul takes refuge, in the shadow of your wings I will take refuge, till the storms of destruction pass by" (Ps. 57:1 ESV). Because of His everlasting lovingkindness, God keeps us close to His heart and protects us from the harsh realities of the sin-cursed world in which we live. He comforts us and by His strong love shelters us from the storms and attacks that would certainly slay us. It's God's steadfast love that keeps Him close to us and ensures our safety.

God's Faithful Love

As we are drawn near to the Lord and find refuge and protection under the shadow of His wings, we will find ourselves immersed in His love. What is this love like? We know that it isn't just one attribute of His being—it is, rather, who He is. That "God is love" (1 John 4:8, 16) should speak comfort and encouragement to us. He doesn't have to remember to put on a love for you. It's His nature to love you and to hide you from destruction. Just as you don't have to remember to breathe, He doesn't have to remember His love and care for you.

One of the most important words describing God's love found in the Old Testament is *hesed*,[1] a word that's used 240 times and speaks primarily of God's lovingkindness. The English Standard Version usually translates this word as "steadfast love," while the King James uses "mercy" or "kindness." Other definitions of *hesed* include grace, faithfulness, goodness, and devotion.[2] This is one of those words that doesn't have a one-to-one translation into English. In fact, we need three English words to properly translate it: strength, steadfastness, and love. Let's take a moment to look at each of the facets of this word so that we can more fully grasp God's disposition toward His children, we who are hiding beneath His wings from the storms that threaten to overwhelm us.

God's Strength Reserved for Us

For me, God's great strength is something that brings encouragement to my heart but also tempts me to see Him as far off or unapproachable. But, when I think that this strength is empowering His love for me, I sense his nearness. His love is one that's empowered by such great endurance that it can't be assailed, swayed, or diminished. It's a mighty compassion that has tied my soul to Him and will keep me safe, under His wings, for all eternity. So, while the emperor penguin father may unwittingly fail to protect his chick from the severe wind, ice, and snow swirling about him, and our family and friends may desert us, our heavenly Father will never fail us. Jesus put it this way: "My sheep hear my voice. . . . and they will never perish; and no one will snatch them out of my hand. My Father, who has given them to me, is greater than all, and no one is able to snatch them out of the Father's hand" (John 10:27–29 ESV).

Think for a moment about the measureless power of our heavenly Father: He declares that His strength is greater than any other and that *no one* could ever to force Him to lift His protection from us. He is greater than any power on earth—whether devils, devilish plans of man, or even our own wickedness—nothing can force His hand open when He has determined to close it. His wing is over you, granting you refuge and protection. Because He is omnipotent—all-powerful—no one is able to change what He has decreed: He's hiding you away from the full force of the storm.

God's Steadfastness for Us

Another facet of God's great love, His *hesed,* has to do with dependability or steadfastness. This crucial element of His love tells us that He will never change His mind about us—loving us one moment and then forsaking us the next. Although each of us has known what it's like to be forsaken—whether by a parent, spouse, child, or friend—in the relationship with our heavenly Father, we'll never be abandoned. Although we discussed this truth in chapter 2, let me remind you of it again.

Even though it's true that we have His precious promise never to leave or forsake us (Heb. 13:5), we also have something else, something that speaks to us dear words that would be unimaginable if they weren't part of the holy Scripture. What we have is the anguished cry of the faithful Son who hung between earth and heaven and exclaimed, "My God, my God, why have you forsaken me?" (Matt. 27:46 ESV). Remember this: for the first time in all eternity, the Father turned His face away from His Son and poured out all of his just and holy wrath upon the innocent Son. The joyous and unbounded fellowship that had existed throughout all time was fractured. The creation recoiled at this breach in cosmic harmony, the earth quaked, the sky was turned dark as night, the veil on the temple mount unraveled. Who could envision such a sight? The One had turned away from His beloved Son!

Again, this portrait is of extraordinary import to each of us. It's important for one simple yet glorious reason: Because He turned away from His Son, He'll never turn away from us! Our loving, faithful Savior was forsaken so that we would never be. We who were God's enemies, who deserved not only to be abandoned but also punished, have been welcomed, forgiven, and tied inseparably to His person.

God's steadfast love is faithful and enduring. Not only does He have the power to remain constant and love us throughout all eternity and against all odds; He also has the disposition of will to do so. He isn't going to change His mind halfway through the storm. The winds may be howling and the rain might be thrashing around us, but our heavenly Father has proclaimed His purposes: *His love is steadfast.* Once our soul has taken refuge under the shadow of His wings, His protection is there for us eternally.

Isaiah prophesied of this love when he said, "Incline your ear, and come to me; hear, that your soul may live; and I will make with you an everlasting covenant, my steadfast, sure love for David" (Isa. 55:3 ESV). The same love that He had for His servant, David, He has for you and me. God declares that His love is steadfast and sure. He isn't changing His mind; His love is constant and resolute. He's made an everlasting covenant—a contract that's based on His *hesed*—He won't desert us in our time of need. Because He has promised not to abandon us, we can "draw near with confidence to the throne of grace, so that we may receive mercy and find grace to help in time of need" (Heb. 4:16).

I know that sometimes, when I'm suffering, I'm tempted to run from the Lord. Rather than drawing near and finding grace, strength, refuge, and steadfast love by His side, I'm tempted to retreat into my self-protective cocoon. I think that I do this because it seems too painful to open up my hurting heart to Him. I imagine that if I can hold my breath long enough and ignore the difficulty, whatever it is, it will pass by. I'm afraid that if I look at or think about my affliction, it will make the pain more unbearable. *If I can just ignore this long enough,* I foolishly think, *I'll make it through. But if I have to think about it, it's liable to overwhelm my soul.* And so I hide.

Even in my sinful self-protection, I can see God's *hesed* extended to me. He wants to transform me. He wants me to change from being a little girl, crouching in some dark corner, licking her wounds, hoping that the storm will pass her by, into a woman of confidence. He isn't interested in my gaining confidence in myself or my own schemes or ability to endure. He doesn't want me to grow strong in myself. What He wants is for me to know Him, to experience His *hesed,* to learn about His nature and person. "Come to Me, all who are weary and heavy-laden, and I will give you rest," the Lord calls to us (Matt. 11:28). Will you come to Him, hide yourself in Him from the storms? He's calling to you today. Don't hide *from* Him; hide yourself *in* Him. It's there you'll find grace and mercy to help in time of need. It's there you'll find His *hesed.*

God's Love for Us

Even though everything we've learned about *hesed* is glorious, there are still rich treasures in this word. God's disposition toward us isn't merely one of strength or dependability. His disposition toward us is one of love. This might seem to be such a truism that it almost goes without saying. After all, as we said, God is love. Almost everything we know about God, beginning at those verses we may have first read at a football game, "For God so loved the world that He gave . . ." (John 3:16), speak of His love. And yet, as we walk through dark storms, sometimes even this light can be dimmed. God loves His people. His love isn't mere sentimentalism or saccharine well wishes. No, His love is active and jealous.

Hesed may be best related to the thought of marital love. In any marriage, love is certainly a legal matter, "and there are legal sanctions for infractions. Yet the relationship, if sound, far transcends mere legalities."[3] Does my husband have a legal responsibility toward me and I toward him? Yes, of course. Do we both have spiritual commitments also? Yes. But our marriage is more than a mere legal agreement and prior commitments. It is a deep, heartfelt compassion and devotion that we have toward each other. What we have is more than a legal agreement to love each other, although it is that. It is also a frame of heart that says that our lives are wholly devoted to the good of the other. This is the kind of love the Lord has for you.

The idea of God's marital devotion toward His people is captured by the prophet Hosea, who speaks on God's behalf to his faithless wife, Israel: "I will betroth you to Me forever; Yes, I will betroth you to Me in righteousness and in justice, in lovingkindness and in compassion, And I will betroth you to Me in faithfulness. Then you will know the LORD" (Hos. 2:19–20).

In these verses we can see the Lord's *hesed* for His people. Words like *forever, lovingkindness,* and *faithfulness* illustrate His generous heart. Even though we're so frequently like that unfaithful wife whose "loyalty is like a morning cloud and . . . the dew which goes away early" (Hos. 6:4), His steadfast love is forever faithful and overflowing. This is the nature of the love that your Lord has for you! Can you take refuge in Him? Will He welcome you and protect you? Of course! His love is that great!

Strong and Steadfast Lovingkindness

One of the most precious passages about God's love is found in Romans 8, particularly the last few verses. I know that you're probably familiar with these words, but I'd like to encourage you to read them again in light of the truths we've been discussing. To help you make this more personal, I've slightly amplified a portion of Romans 8. We don't want to miss the fact that God's love extends to *all* His people, but I do want to you be sure that you're including yourself in the beloved. Read this passage aloud and take to heart the marital promises He's making to you:

> Who shall separate me from the love of Christ, my Husband? Shall tribulation, or distress, or persecution, or famine, or nakedness, or danger, or sword? No, in all these things I am more than a conqueror because of His great love for me I am sure that neither death nor life, nor angels nor rulers, nor things present nor things to come, nor powers, nor height nor depth, nor anything else in all creation, will be able to separate me from the love of God in Christ Jesus our Lord.

When you feel as though the gale is blowing so fiercely that you'll be plucked from your refuge under His wings, remember—nothing in all creation is strong enough to separate you from your omnipotent God! When all the forces of hell seem to be raging about you—in your body, heart, or mind—when you can't trust in your own ability to keep yourself securely tucked away under his wings, remember: no one and nothing is able to pry His hand open or keep you from His love. You will persevere because of His invincible love. You don't have to depend on your ability to hold on, keep a good confession, or have steadfast faith. He's got you—you're safe—and nothing, no earthly affliction, supernatural beings, distances, or anything else in all of His creation is stronger than His love! Let's rejoice in that steadfast love! Let's run toward it and find His comfort and strength!

God's Comforting Love

Isaiah spoke thus of God's love, "As one whom his mother comforts, so I will comfort you; and you will be comforted" (Isa. 66:13). Even though God usually refers to Himself as a Father, in this consoling metaphor, He says that He's like a mother who comforts her children. As we're hidden safely away, under His wing, experiencing His warmth and hearing His heart, He conveys sweet joys and delights to our soul. "I will comfort you; and you will be comforted," He promises.

At the time of this writing, I have four grandchildren with two more on the way (yippee!). I know I'm blessed. Not only am I blessed to live to see my children's children; I'm also blessed because they live close by and I get to see them frequently. What a joy! So, even though I'm old enough to get letters from AARP (which I promptly toss), I also have lots of opportunities to watch my daughters comfort their children, and sometimes I even get in on the fun. Although I hate to see my darlings suffer in any way, I have to admit that I love to comfort them. "Oh, no!" I exclaim. "Did you get a boo-boo? Come and let Mimi make it better." And then I pick them up and snuggle them in close to me, and I pray for them and stroke their little heads and whisper words of consolation in their sweet little ears. "You'll be all right, my love. Jesus is here, and He'll make it better."

I wonder if the Lord loves comforting us as much as we love comforting our children or grandchildren. I'll bet He does. I'll bet that He loves gathering us close to Him and looking into our faces with compassion and kindness and speaking soothing words of consolation to our hearts: "You'll be all right, my love. I'm here, and I'll make it better."

He Comforts Us in Our Afflictions

The Lord does love to comfort us. I'm sure that the joy that we get from comforting others has to be part of His image in us. Something this good surely didn't spring from our own heart, did it? No, I know that He's a God of comfort. How does He bring us that sense of His nearness, His comfort and strength? He does so in a number of ways. First, God comforts us by giving us grace to persevere through trial. Paul wrote of this comfort:

> No temptation has overtaken you that is not common to man. God is faithful, and he will not let you be tempted beyond your ability, but with the temptation he will also provide the way of escape, that you may be able to endure it. (1 Cor. 10:13 ESV)

He has promised to be with us in each of our trials. Sometimes, in the midst of difficulty, we're tempted to ask, "Where is God?" This verse brings us the comforting reassurance that we need: God is faithful, and He won't let us be tempted beyond our ability to endure. He hasn't left us or laid something on our backs that He won't enable us to bear. That's not to say that our burdens are always easy to see through and that we'll always be able to skip along no matter what befalls us.

As I was writing this, I received news that a friend, a young, strong firefighter and father of three, has been diagnosed with stage 3 cancer. We don't know what the future holds. I don't even know what to say to him as we're all reeling from his news. The only thing that I do know is that God has him tucked away, in the place of refuge and that He hasn't placed on him anything more than he can handle. I have to admit that, in some ways, that seems easy to say and fairly hard to live out. How is this precious family supposed to bear up under this trial? My only answer to this question is that God is faithful. My faith can't be based on anything other than His word, no matter what the doctors say about percentages for recovery or what my faithless heart says about the future. His word tells me that He is faithful and has promised to give us a place of escape from the fiery trial: under His wings, taking refuge there. Sometimes hiding under His wings means believing that when you pray, "God help me and hide me," He's done it. "I know you're here, O Lord; let me know your grace!" And then, as seconds become minutes and minutes become days that blossom out into a lifetime, we see that He's done what we didn't think He could do. He's been faithful, sustained us in our affliction, He's enabled us to endure what we thought we could never endure.

God also comforts us by granting us the ability to do what He calls us to do even when we don't think we can. Paul's benediction to the Thessalonians reads, "Now may our Lord Jesus Christ Himself and God our Father, who has loved us and given us eternal comfort and good hope by grace, comfort and strengthen your hearts in every good work and word" (2 Thess. 2:16–17).

God's comfort is meant not only to speak peace into our souls, "It will be okay, I'm here;" but also to infuse us with the power we need to follow and obey Him, even when His path leads us down into a lion's den or up onto a garden mount. God's comforting grace not only protects us from the ravages of the storm; it also infuses us with the power that we need to stand. This power is efficacious even when what we'd like to do is throw off the faith, squirm out of His grasp, and cry out for the rocks to fall on us.

You see, His comfort is far more than loving words meant to make us feel better. It's a grace that's meant to evidence itself in every "good work and word." What is the good work and word that He's calling you to today? Perhaps it's merely a whispered prayer, "I know He sees me. I know He's here. Father, I come to you." Or is it something more? Perhaps it's an act of faith: "I'll call a friend and ask for help," or "I'll write a letter to a fellow sufferer," or "I'll pour out to someone else even though I don't feel like I have enough for myself."

I don't know what good work or word He's got for you today. But I do know this: His comfort is meant to enable you to do what He's calling you to do; to place one foot in front of another by faith. His comfort will sustain you and enable you to take one breath and then another, to cause those breaths to form words of reliant prayer. "Father, in you my soul takes refuge, in the shadow of your wings I will take refuge. Oh, God! Have mercy on me!" And then, as you're invigorated with His sustaining comfort, He'll open your eyes to the suffering around you and give you a word to sustain the needy (Prov. 12:18). Do you feel that you're too weak to sustain another person? That's good, because when you're weak that's when others will know His strength through you. You don't have the resources others need in yourself, but you do have His comfort and this consolation that you'll be giving to another. Here's His promise: "The LORD sustains all who fall and raises up all who are bowed down" (Ps. 145:14).

What is He calling you to do today? What is the act of faith that His comfort is meant to enable you to do? He's hiding you there beneath the shadow of His wings, infusing you with strength. What does His nearness empower you to do right now?

His Expected and Unexpected Arrivals

There are times when God's comfort comes to us supernaturally, through an illumination of the heart, when all of a sudden, out of the blue, you just know that the Lord is with you, sheltering you under His wings. I've had experiences like that, and if you've walked with Him for any time at all, I'm sure you have, too. Sometimes I've felt them in prayer or while reading a passage of Scripture. The light comes on—verses that I've read hundreds of times spring to life and I know that I'm hearing the soothing voice of my Savior. "I'm hiding you; I'm keeping you from these storms. They'll soon pass you by."

There have been other times, though, when God's presence visits me when I'm not looking for it. Unannounced and unforeseen He comes to me, and I'm like Jacob, who discovers he's made his bed in the house of God and didn't know it! "Surely the LORD is in this place, and I did not know it. . . . How awesome is this place! This is none other than the house of God, and this is the gate of heaven. . . . He called the name of that place Bethel" (Gen. 28:16–17, 19).

There have been days when I've been slogging along, trying to make it through and keep the hounds of pain, doubt, and despair at bay when, all of a sudden, I discover that instead of being in Wal-Mart, I'm in Bethel! "You're here, aren't you, Lord?" I whisper. "Thank you for your kindness to remind me that I'm not alone, even though my thoughts were far away from you."

These unexpected visits are dear to me because they're reminders of His steadfast love. He's with me even when I'm not aware of Him; His love is powerful and unfailing. These surprises are special because they serve to remind me that His presence isn't based on my ability to sustain a constant and unflagging faith or even when I'm obedient and in prayer. His presence is with me when I'm thinking of Him, bowing in compliant worship and supplication, and He's with me when all I care about is finding the aisle with the diapers and hoping they have the right size. He doesn't visit me because my love is steadfast. No, He visits me because *His love is steadfast.*

His Comfort Comes to Me through You

God frequently moves supernaturally, making us aware of His presence through a verse, a prayer, a sunrise, a surprise visit. He can and does move supernaturally, by His Spirit, to illumine our hearts to His truth and imminence. I've discovered that one of the most blessed results of being in the storm is the experience of His soothing presence. Is it the same for you?

I've also learned that although His presence does come to me supernaturally and at times unexpectedly, it also comes to me through concrete and ordinary means. So, while it is true that the Lord can and sometimes does move by His Spirit, He also uses specific methods to bless His children. Let's look particularly at one of these means: fellowship with other believers.

We all know the story of Job. He was afflicted by his enemy, with the full permission of His loving Father. In the midst of the overwhelming anguish of his soul, when the heavens seemed to reflect the hardness he feared was in his heavenly Father's heart, when everything he then knew about the God he loved and served was being turned upside down, he longed for the comfort that friends would bring him. He said, "For the despairing man there should be kindness from his friend; so that he does not forsake the fear of the Almighty" (Job 6:14).

Do you feel like Job today? Do you fear you're about to drown in a dismal pit of depression and sorrow? Are you terrified that your weakness will overcome you and that you'll forsake the "fear of the Almighty"? You're not alone. Would it surprise you to hear that the great apostle Paul, whose intense faith and ardent zeal planted churches and persevered through intense affliction, wrote, "God, who comforts the depressed, comforted us by the coming of Titus" (2 Cor. 7:6)? Paul was in such a trial that he needed the good news and dear fellowship that his friend Titus brought him. As Paul had sweet communion with Titus and heard of the Lord's work in the Corinthian church, he was encouraged to remember God's great power in His present circumstance. God comforts the depressed through other believers.

Both Job and Paul expected God's comfort to arrive through the avenue of their friends. They knew that the Lord frequently uses other believers to bring consolation to the afflicted soul. Do you drink deeply of the wine of His comfort poured out to you by His servants? Have you enjoyed their loving touch, their grace-filled words, their prayer?

Again, it seems as though there is a great temptation to hide when I'm hurting. When I don't want to talk about "it" again, being around people who want to minister to me and draw me out, seems in some ways to just make "it" worse. When my friends ask me, "How are you doing?" what should I say? Should I say that I'm afraid that I'm about to forsake the fear of the Almighty? Should I say, "I'm fine. Really. Thanks for asking"? I think that the best response is a simple and humble confession. *"It's hard for me to answer your questions right now. I'm struggling and talking about my struggle makes it seem worse to me. I know you're trying to love and comfort me, and I'm truly thankful for that. Would you please just continue to pray for me and feel free to share with me anything you think that the Lord wants you to share?"* In answering this way, you're asking to be excused from running through every detail again, but you're not cutting yourself off from God's soothing touch.

It may be that you feel that the answer I've suggested above is more than you can say. Please feel free to pare it down to whatever you think you can say, but don't cut yourself off from others. Remember and believe that God is a God of comfort, and one of the primary methods He'll use to console you is the words and prayers of other believers.

Although it is true that one of the hallmarks of affliction is a sense of isolation, and although it is also true that your brothers and sisters can't fully enter into your suffering, God has placed them near you to be one of the means He will use to wrap His wings of refuge around you. You feel isolated and alone, I know. Please let me strongly encourage you not to compound this sense of alienation by hiding from the help and fellowship of others whom God is calling to serve you. God has placed His Son's bride there by you. He's surrounded you with His steadfast lovingkindness, and His *hesed* will come to you through many avenues. I imagine that what you're looking for is complete deliverance from this pain and affliction. I don't know whether that's His plan for you or not. But I do know that the church has been given to you by your loving Father to sustain, encourage, strengthen, and console you during your bitter winter trek.

The March of Saints

There are so many ways that we're like that helpless penguin chick, so dependent, so weak, in so much need of the refuge that only our Father can give us. I know that there are probably times when you assay your faith and doubt whether you'll make it past this dark winter. It's easy to look at the storms of destruction that assail us and to think, *These storms are never going to end!* When the wind is howling around us, it seems impossible to remember the gentle breezes of a spring day. The baby penguin who's hatched in the midst of the most severe weather on earth doesn't know that the sun can shine and that there are seas full of yummy fish and that one day he'll leave the forsaken place of his birth and swim through waters of plenty. All he knows is the storm and his father's warmth, and for him, at that moment, that's enough. Of course, the reality is that the emperor penguin may die trying to protect his young. We, too, have a Savior who died, but His death *guarantees* our victory. He was promised that He would "see His offspring" (Isa. 53:10). This precious joy was assured to Him by His Father, and nothing is going to prevent that from happening. Just think, if He was willing to suffer and die for your soul, will He let your faith freeze to death on the icy field of affliction? Of course not!

Will His near presence be enough for you and me? I'm confident that it will. It will because He's promised us His powerful and faithful lovingkindness. He'll keep us safe and warm until the storms of destruction pass by. And pass us by they will. That, of course, is the sustaining hope of all believers. When we suffer, we don't suffer like the world, for we have hope that even if this affliction never leaves us here on this earth, we won't be here, forever. This isn't all there is. We have His assurance that a day will come when all the suffering and anguish we've known here will be transformed into joy, and the shadows that terrified us here are shown to be what they were all along: merely the shadow of His wings. "Comfort us and grant us trusting hearts, oh, Lord," we pray. "We take refuge in the shadow of your wings."

Finding His Comfort in the Midst of the Storm

1. If you're able, rent and watch the movie *The March of the Penguins* and ask the Lord to open your eyes to the ways that He shelters you from the storm.

2. The Old Testament word *hesed* is rich with meaning. It describes the power, faithfulness, and steadfastness of God's lovingkindness to us. The following verses illustrate His *hesed*. As you look them up, pray that He'll open your eyes to the kind of love that He has for you: Psalm 17:7; 23:6; 31:7–8, 16, 21. You could do further study in your concordance, if you like.

The Strong's concordance number for *hesed* is 2617. Although the New Testament doesn't use the Hebrew word *hesed,* God's comfort and mercy aren't absent from the thoughts of the writers. For instance, see Romans 15:5–6; 2 Corinthians 1:3; 2 Thessalonians 2:16–17; 3:3.

3. Can you think of a time when God surprised you with His presence? What comfort or consolation did He bring to you then?

4. Who are the people in your life that God has put there to comfort you? How are you going to seek to be comforted by Him through them in the future? When they ask you, "How are you doing?" what will you say? If you have been avoiding going to church because it's too painful, make that the first act of faith that you'll take. If you're in a church where you don't know anyone, make a point of getting into a small group so that people can speak into your life. Fellowship isn't just for the strong—it's meant specifically for the suffering. See Romans 15:5–6.

5. Summarize the teaching of this chapter in four or five sentences.

His Purpose Fulfilled

I cry out to God Most High, to God who fulfills his purpose
for me. (Ps. 57:2 ESV)

s Phil and I stumbled around in our dark cave of affliction, some of the deepest cuts came from so-called friends and partners who dealt treacherously with us. Feigning friendship and concern, they proceeded behind our backs to try to elevate themselves and crush us. I vividly recall one day, in particular, when I was aching and exhausted and awaiting a flight home after speaking at a women's conference. I called Phil on my cell phone to check in with him and see how he was doing. The words he spoke devastated my heart. "Honey, this is hard to say, and I don't want to upset you, but so-and-so [a trusted friend who had been placed on our board of directors apparently for this purpose] has changed the locks on the business. He's locked

89

me out." What? Phil, locked out of his own business? The business he'd worked for years and years to build? How could this happen? What was God doing? Where was He?

At that moment, I could relate with David's words as he fled from Saul. David's descriptions of his afflictions were vivid: he felt he was being engulfed in a storm of destruction (v. 1). He believed he was being trampled upon (v. 3) and that his soul was in the midst of fiery beasts! These weren't actual beasts that he could kill with a sword or a spear; these were men who were tormenting him (v. 4). These men had mouths filled with devastation, teeth like spears and arrows, who spoke words that were like sharp swords, jabbing and slicing at David's heart.

The malignant speech that spewed relentlessly from these ruthless enemies was like a contaminating venom that had even found its way into David's virtuous soul. "My soul is in the midst of lions . . . my soul was bowed down," he moaned. This faithful servant found himself so assailed by the lies of his adversaries that he was tempted to renounce his integrity and take matters into his own hands. I know that temptation all too well. I can hear the fiendish enticement, can't you?

> Listen, David, you're being accused of wanting to commandeer the throne, aren't you? The one you served, Saul, is saying that you're an ambitious, disloyal, conspiring usurper. Here you are, trying to be so good, so righteous, and all the while your powerful enemy is persecuting you to the dust! Why do you hold on to your integrity, David? Saul thinks you're trying to kill him anyway—that's what he's telling everyone—so why not just go ahead and do it? After all, hasn't God said that you're going to be king, so why not make that happen? Oh, and, by the way, where is your God? Is this how He repays you for all your righteousness?

I'll admit that there have been days when I've heard that kind of diabolical refrain myself. Of course, my circumstances were different. I wasn't being tempted to slit anyone's throat, but I was heinously tempted to murder our betrayers with my tongue. I'll admit honestly that there were times that if I could have made them disappear (without killing them), I might have. I was tempted to slander, gossip, vengeance, and bitterness. In my heart, I secretly plotted ways I might repay those who had treated us so treacherously and pondered how they deserved to be punished. I daydreamed about a time when I might triumph over them. Yes, I've been tempted in these same ways.

For you, the temptation you're facing might be something different. Perhaps you're battling ongoing pain and disease, and you're tempted to abandon your faith. Every jab of pain, every sleepless night is another chorus in the seemingly never-ending refrain: *God's not good; you're serving Him for nothing; you're not going to make it to the end!* Maybe what you're facing isn't a life-threatening disease but rather a degenerative condition that will eventually confine you to a wheelchair. *Will life be worth living then? How could I stand the humiliation of having someone else bathe me or change my diaper? How could I subject my loved ones to such an existence? Perhaps I should just pray that God would end my life now, like Job did.*[1]

Perhaps you've had days and days of bitter conflict with a spouse or a child. *I can't take this anymore!* you might be thinking. *One more day of this conflict, and I'm going to have to get out of here before I lose my mind!*[2] It may be that you're facing financial ruin and your propensity would be to cut corners or fudge on the truth or to angrily blame your spouse or your employer for your situation. Or maybe you long to be married or have children and even though you've sought to keep a good testimony of God's faithfulness, your enemy is holding the clock up to your ear and you're beginning to wonder whether you'll be able to fight off the hounds of hell that are baying at the gates of your heart: *Go ahead and marry an unbeliever; God isn't keeping up His part of this bargain, why should you?* Or, *if God isn't going to give you children, then you should live selfishly and luxuriously, spending all your extra time and money on making your life here enjoyable.* Can't you hear your enemy's lies?

"If Only. . . ." The Endless Refrain

While I was writing this chapter, I had the opportunity to spend the day with my dearest friend, Julie, of whom I spoke in the introduction. This month marked the two-year anniversary of her son, Richard's, death. "How is it for you now?" I asked her. Tears began to stream down her face, and I had my answer. Her loss is a relentless pain that seeks to fill the void where Richard had been. How can a mother find solace in a world where her child is missing? *It's all your fault,* the tempter suggests. *If only you had just stopped him from going out the door . . . if only you had just said this, or not done that . . . if only you had been a better mother or . . .* day after day his vile lies infect her heart until she loses sight of God's goodness and sovereignty and all she can see is her failure and emptiness. Have you heard these lies before? Our enemy finds fiendish delight in accusing us of sins and demeaning God's steadfast love. If he could murder us and our faith, he would.

What's our enemy up to? What's his purpose in our storms? He wants us to think thoughts too low of God and too high of second causes.[3] *It's all your fault!* he screams in my ear. *You're a failure, a disgrace; everything that's happened to you happened because you're such a sinner!* Or if that doesn't work as he'd planned, he changes his tack and says, *The people around you are such failures! Every affliction you're facing is because of them!* This is how I'm tempted to think when I hurt. But, when I foolishly assign blame (either to myself, Satan, or others), I'm failing to recognize that the person who is sinning against me, and even Satan, is *under the Lord's sovereign control.* Even Satan, our powerful enemy, is merely, as Luther said, "a mad dog on a chain." He does bark and growl and would seek to bite and devour us, but God is holding tight his leash. So whether he's directly accusing me or enticing others to "set a net for my steps" as David said (Ps. 57:6 ESV), God is overseeing everything in my life—that He might fulfill every purpose He has for my life. When it comes to achieving His goal, God isn't worried. He'll fulfill every purpose of His, and He might even use His mad dog to help accomplish that.

"Now's Your Chance!"

It wasn't merely the tempter who was speaking to David's heart, there in that dark cavern; it was also his own men. When King Saul had gone into the cave to relieve himself, David's men seized their opportunity and sought to encourage David to take matters into his own hands. "Here is the day of which the LORD said to you, 'Behold, I will give your enemy into your hand, and you shall do to him as it shall seem good to you'" (1 Sam. 24:4 ESV),[4] they said. Perhaps they thought they were giving him godly counsel, or perhaps they knew their counsel was rooted in evil ambition and the desire to triumph over their enemy. In any case, their advice found its mark in David's besieged heart. The hellish goading of his enemy and his friends washed over him until he finally succumbed and "arose and cut off the edge of Saul's robe" (1 Sam. 24:4). David could have slit Saul's throat, but he refrained and perhaps, in the midst of his temptation, he reasoned that this little action wasn't anything much. It was, after all, the lesser of two evils. But, even so, evil it was. At this act of rebellion, if it weren't for God's restraining hand, his men might have fallen on Saul and murdered him there. David had sinned, and that sin might have borne toxic fruit in the lives of his followers.[5]

His Grace Is Even Here

The following verses ought to bring us all great comfort and encouragement. Even though David was running for his life, being slandered, dreadfully tempted, and even succumbed to sin, God was there with him. Bathe your soul in these delightful words, "And afterward, David's heart struck him" (1 Sam. 24:5 ESV). God didn't desert David in his severe temptation and failure. God sent from heaven and saved him! After he had sinned, the Holy Spirit did His faithful and effective work of convicting David of sin and teaching him the right way to go. I can imagine that at this moment, David may have felt alone and inadequate. Perhaps he was listening to the voice of the tempter: *How are you ever going to be king? You're supposed to be God's anointed one, but look what you've done! You've attacked someone who was anointed by God before you! You'll never make it! You'll never be what God wants you to be! You're such a sinner that He'll never fulfill His purposes for you!* But the beloved presence of God's grace repulsed these treacherous thoughts as His Spirit rushed in and taught David to honor God, even in the dark, and to love his neighbor, though his neighbor was trying to kill him.

His Grace Is Here for You

Earlier I described some possible circumstances that might be plaguing you. Although each of these circumstances and thousands of others like them are heavy burdens to bear, I think that the worst burden of all springs from within ourselves. Isn't this the way that our accuser brings our sins before us? John the Revelator called our enemy "the accuser of our brethren . . . he who accuses them before our God day and night" (Rev. 12:10). Satan takes cruel delight in rehearsing your sins before you, not so that you will come to repentance but so that you'll be focused on yourself, your weakness, your unworthiness, all in the hopes that your testimony and faith will fail and God's purpose won't be fulfilled.

If that's your experience, if you find that you think more on your failures and sins than on God's great power to love and effectively save, then Psalm 57 has good news for you. Here it is: "I will cry out . . . to God who fulfills His purpose for me. He will send from heaven and save me; he will put to shame him who tramples on me" (Ps. 57:2–3 ESV).

God has proclaimed that He will fulfill His purpose for you and me. God is now and always will be directly involved in seeing that all of His holy will is accomplished. What is His purpose for you? Nothing less than remaking you to be like His Son (Rom. 8:28–29)! Amazing, isn't it? His purpose isn't just that you make it through to the end, frantically grasping the frayed edges of your faith by the tips of your fingers. No, it's that you'll be transformed into the likeness of Jesus Christ!

I know that when I'm faced with my great inconsistencies,

sin, and folly, the thought that He's going to make me into the image of His Holy Son seems laughable. I'm going to be like Him? He's going to fulfill His purpose in me? If you're like me, you might need to ponder what He's said about how committed He is to His own purposes:

- "Brethren beloved by the Lord . . . God has chosen you from the beginning for salvation through sanctification by the Spirit and faith in the truth" (2 Thess. 2:13). You were chosen before time began for salvation through His transforming power!
- "After you have suffered for a little while, the God of all grace, who called you to His eternal glory in Christ, will Himself perfect, confirm, strengthen and establish you" (1 Peter 5:10). He "personally will come and pick you up, and set you firmly in place, and make you stronger than ever" (TLB).
- "For God has not destined us for wrath, but for obtaining salvation through our Lord Jesus Christ, who died for us, so that . . . we will live together with Him" (1 Thess. 5:9–10). God's purpose for you is not wrath but salvation, so that you can be with Him!
- "In Him also we have . . . been predestined according to His purpose who works all things after the counsel of His will, to the end that we who were the first to hope in Christ would be to the praise of His glory" (Eph. 1:10–12). Everything in your life is working according to His will so that you will become a woman who brings praise to Him!

- "And we know that God causes all things to work together for good to those who love God, to those who are called according to His purpose. For those whom He foreknew, He also predestined to become conformed to the image of His Son, so that He would be the firstborn among many brethren; and these whom He predestined, He also called; and these whom He called, He also justified; and these whom He justified, He also glorified" (Rom. 8:28–30).

Look at that last passage again, will you? God is so sure that He's going to fulfill His purpose in you, in making you into the image of His Son, that He talks about it as if it were already complete. If you're in Christ today, then He already speaks of you as being predestined, called, justified, *and* glorified! He is sure that you're going to be where He wants you to be when He wants you to be there. He's sure about it because He's going to make it happen; nothing and no one (not even you!) can forestall any of His purposes!

The wonderful truth of our God's sustaining grace should give us hope to cry out to God as David did. It should also give us hope to believe that we'll see the work he's promised to do in our life. It's easy to think that we aren't growing the way we should be because we're bogged down in some affliction that seems to be occupying all of our attention. I know that it's easy to say, "If this trial were not part of my life, I could get on with the real business of Christianity." Of course, the truth is, this is the real business of Christianity! The affliction itself, coupled with your failures and successes in it, are the instruments that the Lord uses to strengthen, sustain, and change you. Not only this trial but also your response to this trial is part of His sweet transformation in your life.

I Cry Out to God

During the darkest months of our trial, Phil and I learned what it meant to cry out to God. On that flight home, when all I could see was treachery and devastation, I didn't even know how to pray. All I was sure of was that there was a God who ruled in the hearts and affairs of men and that He heard my cry.

This has been the experience of every believer who's ever lived through the dark night of the soul. I love the way that David phrases his experience, "I cry out to God Most High, to God who fulfills His purpose for me" (Ps. 57:2 ESV). David's use of the title "God Most High" is significant, considering the fact that he was being hunted down by the highest ruler in the land, King Saul. David was acknowledging that Saul had authority, but the God to whom he cried had more.

It's important for us to take a little journey into the Hebrew that David employed when addressing his prayer. In the English Standard Version we're told that he cried out to "God Most High (*El Elyon*) and to God (*Elohim*)." It would be easy to miss the rich treasures that these two distinct names display, and I know that the Lord would want to reveal Himself to you in a way that would build your faith, especially in light of your present circumstance or personal sin.

Who was it that David was imploring for salvation? It was God Most High, *El Elyon*. *El Elyon* is the name that the Lord uses to designate Himself as the sovereign ruler of all the universe. He's "a great King over all the earth [who] . . . subdues peoples

. . . and nations" (Ps. 47:2–3), and He's the one who alone is "Most High over all the earth" (Ps. 83:18).

You and I can speak and pray and hope for the best, but it is only *El Elyon* "who speaks and it comes to pass. . . .[it is] from the mouth of [*El Elyon*] that both good and ill go forth" (Lam. 3:37–38)! We can pray confidently to God Most High, because whatever He has decreed will come to pass. Has He declared that He *will* fulfill all His purposes for you? Then He will. He has the power and authority to follow through on every good plan in His heart. After King Nebuchadnezzar's reason returned to him, he knew who the highest-ranking King was. He said of Him, "all the inhabitants of the earth are accounted as nothing, but He does according to His will in the host of heaven and among the inhabitants of the earth; and no one can ward off His hand or say to Him, 'What have You done?'" (Dan. 4:35). Since *El Elyon* rules sovereignly over all rulers, it follows that He can also overrule in the lives of his beloved children.

If God Is Sovereign, Why Pray?

I once had a conversation with a friend who was debating whether she believed that God is truly sovereign or not. To put a finer point on it, she asked me why she should pray if God is sovereign and ruling over every facet of His universe. I answered her by asking her another question, "If God isn't sovereign, why pray?" We both looked at each other and laughed. The truth is that every person who prays that God would save a soul or heal a body or provide a job has to believe that He rules sovereignly over the hearts and minds of all people. Otherwise, why pray?[6] If God is bound by our finite activities and desires, then how could He ever answer our cries?

You can pray confidently, as David did, for mercy and salvation. We're invited cry out to God Most High, and we don't have to worry about anything getting in the way of His good plan for our lives. No demonic power or stubbornness of heart can frustrate His plan for us (Isa. 14:24, 27). It's true that sometimes God's plan is not our own and we find that our prayers are not answered as we'd like. As much as we know God's will, we're to pray according to it, but there are obviously times when we don't know His plan, when His will is secret, and during those times we're always to add the caveat, "Thy will be done" to our prayer. But even in light of our finite knowledge, we can assume that because God is a loving and holy Father, it's *always* His will save and be merciful to us in whatever way will best achieve His purpose in our lives. Sometimes, His purpose is fulfilled by answering no to our cries. At this point in David's life, God answered no to his hopes to be freed from Saul's persecution. God did bring a short season of relief to him, but it wasn't time for the battle to be over. Even though He sometimes says no, you and I will never hear the divine negative when we're praying for His grace, strength, mercy, and help to ultimately sustain our soul through a difficult trial or even through our struggle with sin.[7]

The other title that David uses to address is prayer is *Elohim*. *Elohim* is translated "God" in our English Bibles, but it brings with it the thought of great potency and strength. It is the primary Hebrew word translated "God" in the Old Testament and is the title that God uses to designate Himself as our Creator.

We first read of *Elohim* in Genesis 1:1, "In the beginning [*Elohim*] created the heavens and the earth." The one to whom David was praying for help was the one who spoke and the worlds leaped into existence. This is no puny god who might or might not be able to come to David's rescue! This was *Elohim*, the Creator of all! He can create worlds that we're still not aware of, and He can create a willing and holy heart within you, too. He can easily create the storms, and He can effortlessly calm them, working all things for His ultimate purposes in your life.

In addition, *Elohim* is a plural noun. Many scholars believe that the plural form of this word is an Old Testament evidence that the one God is trinitarian in nature:

> In the New Testament God revealed that He is not only one but a family of persons—an eternal, inexhaustible, and dynamic triune family of Father, Son, and Holy Spirit, who are one in will and purpose, love and righteousness.[8]

You can rejoice because the Father, Son, and Spirit are one in will and purpose! What is our trinitarian God's purpose in your life? To conform you to the image of the Son! Will that happen? Yes, of course it will. The Father has decreed that it will be so, the Son has shed His innocent blood to make you His bride, and the Spirit is working relentlessly to transform you. If He can speak and create the world, don't you think he can speak and change you and your circumstance?

Light in the Darkness

On my flight home, I cried and prayed to the Lord. "Oh, God! Please help us. Save us from those who would devour us, and grant us deliverance from the ones who want to tear us to pieces and trample us. Be merciful to us, O Lord! We're hiding ourselves in you."

When Phil picked me up at the airport and I was safely hidden away in the car, I wept. And then, the Lord's grace came to me, and I remembered that we were not alone in this humiliating betrayal. He reminded me of the Son who loved our souls unimaginably more than I could ever ask or think, who had been betrayed and humiliated for me. He had been betrayed by His own. One of the Twelve sold Him, and even those who truly loved Him fled from Him. His beloved disciple, Peter, denied that he even knew Him. And then He was exposed to the humiliation of a mock trial, He was taunted and stripped and beaten. He hung naked on a cursed tree and was jeered at by religious leaders, common soldiers, and a robber. He endured all this to fulfill His purpose for you and for me. Instead of weeping over the hardness and treacherousness of our friends, we should have been weeping over the hardness and treachery in our own hearts, while at the same time rejoicing in what a love like Christ's meant. In that moment we knew that we were going to be all right. God was going to fulfill His purposes in us. Since He had already sent from heaven and saved us from the most daunting and significant problem we had, our sin and separation from Him, we knew that He would, when it pleased His gracious will to do to so, deliver us from the children of men. This is the God you serve! *El Elyon, Elohim,* the sovereign King of all creation who loves you and shelters you under His mighty wings. Don't despair, dear friend. He's here.

Finding His Comfort in the Midst of Your Storm

1. What are the lies that the tempter is whispering to you? What is his counsel to you? Is he telling you to sinfully take matters into your own hands? Is he telling you that

you're such a sinner that even though God would love to bless you He can't? After pondering the verses below, write out how you will answer his accusations: Ephesians 1:10–12; 1 Thessalonians 5:9–10; 2 Thessalonians 2:13; 1 Peter 5:10; Romans 8:28–30.

2. The story of Peter's denial and subsequent restoration should bring great hope to you as you survey your responses to this storm and reckon with your unworthiness to receive His love and grace. You can read this story in Matthew 26:30–75; Luke 22:31–62; John 21:11–19. The Lord fulfilled His purpose in Peter's life, despite Peter's weaknesses and sins. Do you believe that He'll do the same for you?

3. In the following verses God is designated by His name, *El Elyon*. What do you learn about the sovereign Ruler of all from each one? How do these truths encourage you in your storm? Psalms 47:2–3; 78:35; 83:18; 91:1–9; 97:9.

4. In the following verses God is designated by His name, *Elohim*. What do you learn about the Creator, trinitarian God from each one? How do these truths encourage you in your storm? Genesis 1; Exodus 12:12; 14:19; Psalms 4:1; 18:28ff.

5. Summarize what you've learned in this chapter in three or four sentences.

Our Hearts Grow Strong

My heart is steadfast, O God, my heart is steadfast! . . .
For your steadfast love is great to the heavens, your faithfulness
to the clouds. (Ps. 57:7, 10 ESV)

One Christmas during our stormy years, my friend, Bev, gave me a beautiful calendar containing a picture of a different lighthouse every month.[1] Although I'd been aware of the well-known spiritual metaphor of the lighthouse—Christ shining out to guide our lives safely to shore—I don't think that I'd ever appreciated the hardiness of the lighthouse or its keeper until I spent time really looking at these photographs of lighthouses built out in the stormy North Atlantic. Portrait by amazing portrait, I was engulfed by a new and noteworthy metaphor: God had made me like the lighthouse keeper, safely hidden away within the immovable walls of the lighthouse. I did not need to fear the stormy gale that raged around me, as the lighthouse keeper needn't fear the waves that relentlessly battered his home in the sea. My soul was steadfastly protected within the upright tower that had been built by His steadfast love. I could be confident and filled with purposeful praise because I was anchored to the Rock of Ages and nothing would uproot that foundation. Like David, I learned that I could say, "My heart is steadfast, O God, my heart is steadfast!" because His "steadfast love is great to the heavens [and His] faithfulness to the clouds" (Ps. 57:7, 10 ESV).

It's appropriate for us to use the metaphor of a lighthouse when thinking about our steadfast heart, because the word for "steadfast" (*kuwn*) comes from a Hebrew root word that means "being firmly established and . . . firmly anchored."[2] This wonderful word succinctly portrays both the firm anchor that fastens the lighthouse to rocks in depths of the ocean and the steadfast resolution and faith that animate our hearts to worship God even now, in the eye of our stormy gale.

If this were a fictional book, I would continue on here with my descriptions of how steadfast my heart had grown. I would talk about how strong and stalwart I was, about how nothing fazed me any more because I had such great faith in such a great God. "Look at me—the Lighthouse Woman!" I might sing.

But, alas, the reality is that the transforming work that God began in my life through this trial and by His sanctifying Spirit hasn't been perfected . . . quite yet. And although I firmly believe that His purposes can't be thwarted, I still recognize much weakness and frailty in my heart. That's not to say that I haven't seen any changes—it's just to admit that my heart's transformation from a lean-to made of driftwood and dried palm fronds into a sturdy citadel erected out of durable bricks and anchored to the rock by tempered steel braces hasn't quite happened yet. Like you, I'm in process, and I'm learning to rest in that process, while I strive toward God's goal of steadfastness in my life.

What would a steadfast heart look like? If I had a steadfast heart, would it mean that I was insensible to my afflictions or that I could face any trial, loss, or sorrow without the slightest tremor in my emotions? I don't think so.

The Steadfast Heart of the Lord

If we want to know what perfection of heart looks like, we need to examine the life of the Perfect God-Man, Jesus Christ. Rather than being an impassive, apathetic man who was unexcitable and stoical, He was a man of ardor, fervency, intensity, and emotion. At two times during His earthly ministry He zealously cleared the temple of those who denigrated His Father's house.[3] No onlooker in that crowd would say that Jesus was a stoic. In John 11, we read that He was "deeply moved in His spirit and greatly troubled" (John 11:33 ESV)—so greatly troubled that He wept. D. A. Carson, in commenting on the popular translations of this passage, points out that in fact the Lord was filled with wrath. B. B. Warfield echoes that sentiment:

> What John tells us, in point of fact, is that Jesus approached the grave of Lazarus, in a state, not of uncontrollable grief, but of irrepressible anger. . . . the emotion which tore his breast and clamored for utterance was just rage. . . . It is death that is the object of his wrath, and behind death him who has the power of death, and whom he has come into the world to destroy. Tears of sympathy may fill his eyes. . . . His soul is held by rage.[4]

He wasn't merely saddened by the death of His dear friend. He was furious over the ravages of sin: unbelief, sickness, grief, death. At another occasion we read that when He saw Jerusalem and knew the tribulation that would soon devastate the chosen city, He wept over it (Luke 19:41–46).

Far from being insensible to human emotions, he "actually took upon Him human feelings."[5] When He wept over the coming destruction of Jerusalem, He really did weep—and by this "*weeping* he proved not only that he loved, like a brother, those for whose sake he became man, but also that God made to flow into human nature the Spirit of fatherly love."[6] Isaiah said that He was "a man of sorrows and acquainted with grief" (Isa. 53:3). In addition, on several occasions, Matthew portrayed Him as being "moved with compassion" (Matt. 9:36–38; 14:14–16; 15:32; 20:34). Surely Jesus' heart was warmed with ardor for His people and filled with every sinless sentiment known to man. Our Lord's heart wasn't steadfast because it was insensible to emotional pain. Rather, it was steadfast in spite of how he felt.

We can't leave our treatment of Christ's emotional life without looking at two more passages. In the first, we find our Savior in the Garden of Gethsemane, where He was in agony (Luke 22:44) and was grieved and distressed. His testimony describes His emotional state: "My soul is deeply grieved, to the point of death; remain here and keep watch with Me" (Matt. 26:38). What was the source of such sorrow? Seventeenth century commentator Matthew Henry writes that his soul

> was now in an agony. This proves that Christ had a true human soul; for he suffered, not only in his body, but in his soul. We had sinned both against our own bodies, and against our souls; both had been used in sin, and both had

been wronged by it; and therefore Christ suffered in soul as well as in body. . . .

He was exceedingly sorrowful . . . compassed about with sorrow on all hands. It was sorrow in the highest degree, even unto death; it was a killing sorrow, such sorrow as no mortal man could bear and live. He was ready to die for grief; they were sorrows of death.[7]

Psalm 18:4 speaks prophetically of Christ's burden, "The cords of death encompassed me, and the torrents of ungodliness terrified me." As His pure soul was being infected by torrents of sin and the revolting iniquity of all His elect, He was terrified and excessively burdened.

What does it mean to have a steadfast heart? Does it mean that we never quail before affliction, feel burdened with sorrows, anger, or grief, or are overcome with compassion and pity for those we love? Not at all. Our loving Savior experienced every emotion that we do albeit sinlessly. He felt anger and terror; His heart was overcome by sorrows we've never begun to taste. And yet, He "steadfastly and determinedly set His face to go to Jerusalem" (Luke 9:51 AMP). Even though His soul was greatly troubled, His heart remained steadfast: He was determined to glorify His Father and to drink the cup He had prepared for Him (John 18:11).

Having a steadfast heart doesn't mean that we never exult in joy at God's goodness either. In fact happiness is a sign of godliness! Hebrews 1:9 gives voice to another side of Christ's emotional life. "You have loved righteousness and hated law-lessness; therefore God, Your God, has anointed You with the oil of gladness above Your companions." The gladness that was given to the Son wasn't a saccharine lilt or an impish giggle—it was a full-bodied exuberance and exceeding joy. It was mirth and rejoicing—the kind of rejoicing one does when dancing at a wedding!

The joy and laughter that is part of a godly, steadfast heart was captured beautifully by C. S. Lewis's Christ figure, Aslan. After the first joke occurred in Narnia, Aslan's instruction to the animals was, "Laugh and fear not, creatures. Now that you are no longer dumb and witless, you need not always be grave."[8] Jesus Himself said that His ministry was to bring good news, to "grant those who mourn . . . a garland instead of ashes, the oil of gladness instead of mourning, the mantle of praise instead of a spirit of fainting. So they will be called oaks of righteousness, the planting of the LORD, that He may be glorified" (Isa. 61:3; see also Luke 4:18ff.). This joy and rejoicing are part and parcel of our salvation. It isn't rooted in mere temporal pleasure—it is anchored to the ministry, life, death, and resurrection of the Savior, who "for the joy that was set before him endured the cross" (Heb. 12:2 ESV).

The woman with a steadfast heart is a woman who is alive— alive to all the emotions she's been given by the Lord. She's aware of the sinful possibilities that emotions may enflame, but she's not stoical or afraid to laugh or to cry. She doesn't let her emotions lead her, but she doesn't ignore them either. She can mourn, and she can dance. She can have great joy and hope, and she can fearlessly rejoice when God turns her captivity. A steadfast heart isn't a dead heart; it's a heart that's pulsating with a vibrant, dynamic faith, God-centered thought, and redeemed emotions that bring life and color to every experience.

If having a steadfast heart doesn't mean being emotionless, what does it mean? Let's look again at our psalm and at David's responses to see if we can capture what he meant when he proclaimed, "My heart is steadfast, O God, my heart is steadfast!"

David's Steadfast Heart

In Psalm 57 we see David's progression from pleading to God for mercy, to finding refuge from storms of destruction and treacherous men, and finally on to his confident assertion, "My heart is steadfast. I will sing and make melody!" How did David arrive at this new place of safety and refuge? In the progression of the psalm, the turning point for David seems to be in verse 5, "Be exalted, O God, above the heavens! Let your glory be over all the earth!"

You'll remember that in verse 4, David was praying and bemoaning the present condition of his soul. "My soul is in the midst of lions," he said. Then, in verse 6, he speaks in the past tense, "They set a net for my steps; my soul was bowed down. They dug a pit in my way, but they have fallen into it themselves." It's on the heels of this statement of God's victory that David confidently declares, "My heart is steadfast, O God, my heart is steadfast! I will sing and make melody." What happened to him? Why this change?

David's heart grew steadfast as he began to ponder the magnificent character of his God again. He remembered that he served a God of wisdom: He was wise enough to know how to glorify Himself while achieving David's good. He said, "Your steadfast love is great to the heavens, your faithfulness to the clouds!" He knew that he served a God of love: His love was "great to the heavens"! Although it was so great, it also reached down into his besieged heart. He remembered that his God was faithful. The Lord's faithfulness bridged the great divide from David's dark cavern and up into the clouds. It was impossible that he would ever be abandoned, even though at this moment his trial seemed interminable. As you contemplate the verses that

111

follow, it's my hope that you'll find your soul being assembled, brick by brick, into a resolute fortress; a fortress able to withstand the pounding of any wave.

Think about God's Wisdom

"O Lord, how many are Your works! In wisdom You have made them all; the earth is full of Your possessions" (Ps. 104:24). Everything we see was created through His wisdom. If He can make the starry host and set them to sing joyfully in the heavens, isn't He wise enough to build your life so that it glorifies Him? Remember: In wisdom He shaped the waves that crash against the lighthouse, and it was His wisdom that made the rock that the lighthouse is anchored to.

"Great is our Lord and abundant in strength; His understanding [wisdom] is infinite" (Ps. 147:5). God's wisdom is endless, immeasurable, and vast. I know that it's easy to think that I know best what course my life should take. But when I remember how immeasurable His wisdom is, I know that I have to bow my knee before Him in humble reliance and adoration.

Contemplate Daniel's perspective on the breadth of God's wisdom and the way that His wisdom built Daniel into a man of wisdom, even when he was a captive in a foreign land.

> Daniel said, "Let the name of God be blessed forever and ever, for wisdom and power belong to Him. It is He who changes the times and the epochs; He removes kings and establishes kings; He gives wisdom to wise men and knowledge to men of understanding. It is He who reveals the profound and hidden things; He knows what is in the darkness, and the light dwells with Him. To You, O God of my fathers, I

give thanks and praise, for You have given me wisdom and power." (Dan. 2:20–23)

Look again at the words that Daniel uses to describe God's wisdom and power: He changes the times from one epoch to another. Why? Because it's wise. He elevates one leader and debases another. Why? Because His wisdom is directing Him. Anyone who has knowledge or understanding received it from Him, the fountain of all wisdom. Every secret hidden in the darkness is known and understood fully by Him. And He gives wisdom and power to His children, to make them steadfast and useful in all their afflictions. Take heart, dear sister. God has all the wisdom He needs to bring you to your desired end, and He has all the wisdom you need to know how to make it day by day. No one is outside of His purview; no one can evade His wise providences.

Think about God's Love

How great is His love? David said that His steadfast love (*hesed*) is great even to the heavens. It is not said merely that His love is as high as the heavens but that it is "great to the heavens." C. H. Spurgeon wrote that it was "*high* as the heavens, overtopping the greatest sin, and the highest thought of man. It is *wide* as the far reaching sky, compassing men of all ages, countries and classes. It is *deep* . . . this is deep in abiding foundation."[9]

Paul prayed that the Ephesians would be "rooted and grounded in love, . . .[and] may be able to comprehend . . . the breadth and length and height and depth and to know the love of Christ which surpasses knowledge" (Eph. 3:17–19). Because His love is so high, no storm, no matter how high the elevation of the clouds, can scale it; because it is so broad, no affliction can skirt around it; because it is so deep, no trial can sneak under it. His love is sufficient to keep you steadfastly sheltered from the most extreme misery and hardship because He's already gone through it with you, as Isaiah prophesied, "In all their affliction He was afflicted . . . in His love and in His mercy He redeemed them, and He lifted them and carried them all the days of old" (Isa. 63:9).

Think about God's Faithfulness

The truth of the faithfulness of God strengthens our hearts and makes us steadfast even in the turbulent sea. We can be faithful and steadfast because He will never forsake those who seek Him (Ps. 9:10). Even when our seeking Him amounts to a weak cry for mercy, He's promised that He'll always answer us because we're His. God's pledge do what He's promised to do isn't some minor attribute of the Lord's. God's faithfulness "surrounds" Him—it's the environment in which He lives (Ps. 89:8). Because His word is fixed and sure forever in heaven, His faithfulness to do what He's promised will continue throughout all generations—reaching even unto you and me.

Are these reminders of God's faithfulness, love, and wisdom imparting steadfastness to your soul? I hope so. The one truth that you can anchor your soul into, the one Rock that will sustain you when the winds blow and the floods rise, is that His word teaches us that

> His wisdom will never lead you
> where His love wouldn't want you to go
> and His faithfulness can't keep you.

And so, because He is who He is, your heart, like the mighty lighthouses ensconced securely on craggy outcroppings in the tumultuous sea, can be steadfast.

Also like the lighthouse, your steadfast heart isn't meant to sustain and keep only you. Your steadfast heart is meant to keep others who are being battered by the stormy breakers of life. "Look at her," they say. "If God can sustain her in this, surely He'll sustain me, too." Authentically shining out your belief in God's wisdom, love, and faithfulness doesn't mean that you don't respond emotionally to the surf that threatens to maul your soul. It means that you maintain your determination to praise God and trust deeply in Him no matter what. This is what David said from the cave:

> My heart is steadfast, O God,
>   my heart is steadfast!
> I will sing and make melody!
>   Awake, my glory!
> Awake, O harp and lyre!
>   I will awaken the dawn!
> I will give thanks to you, O Lord, among the
>   people;
>   I will sing praises to you among the nations.
>   (Ps. 57:7–9 ESV)

"When You See Me Worshiping . . ."

A few years ago, I was asked by a group of women in our church to speak to them about how they should handle their discouragements. I talked with them about many of the principles we've been discussing, and I added, "Whenever you see me worshiping, with my hands lifted and my face fully inclined heavenward, you can know that I'm probably fighting discouragement. It's at that time that I'm more intent than ever to express the steadfastness of my trust in Him and most determined to tell my soul to praise Him."

On the Sunday morning after Phil had been locked out of his business, we walked into church together. As the music commenced, the congregation began to sing "Blessed Be Your Name" by Matt and Beth Redman.

On this grievous morning I sang these words in faith as tears poured down my face. Yes, Lord, blessed be your name! You gave to us and you took away—I'm still choosing to say, "Blessed be your Name!" You're that good.

Last month one of the women who had listened to my talk on discouragement reminded me of what I had said that night. She told me that she had been observing my life and that it had helped her remember to steadfastly worship, no matter how she felt. Was I being a lighthouse for her soul? I hope so. I hope that every tear that we shed and every time we bow the knee or lift our hands in humble worship others are taught to trust in the one whose wisdom, faithfulness, and love is powerful enough to build us into strong towers of refuge and safety.

What assurances do we have that our hearts can steadfastly grow into beacons of love, trust, and worship? Do you believe that He can make you into that impenetrable and invulnerable tower in the midst of the raging sea? When I look at my heart, I wonder. But then, I'm reminded that this is God's work and that He is the true Lighthouse. He's the Rock, the one upon whom I'm anchored. He's my fortress and shield, the one who takes the pounding of the bitter waves. He's the Light, the one who shines out the beams of hope and salvation. And He's the one who has promised to faithfully protect and keep us through all eternity.

Finding God's Comfort in the Midst of Your Storm

1. How do you usually respond when you feel the blast of wind on your face? Are you sad, angry, questioning, or fearful? Remember that emotional responses are not necessarily sinful in themselves, but they can be sinful if you allow them to tempt you to respond to your affliction in ungodly ways. What is your pattern of response? How might it change to reflect Christ's emotional responses? The following messianic psalms are meant to help you see how Christ suffered and how He responded: Psalms 69:1–3; 116:3–4; 40:7–12.

2. Commentator Matthew Henry wrote the following on Matthew 26, your Savior's struggle in Gethsemane: "He had a full and clear prospect of all the sufferings that were before him. He foresaw the treachery of Judas, the unkindness of Peter, the malice of the Jews, and their base ingratitude. He knew that he should now in a few hours be scourged, spit upon, crowned with thorns, nailed to the cross; death in its most dreadful appearances, death in pomp, attended with all its terrors, looked him in the face; and this made him sorrowful, especially because it was the wages of our sin, which he had undertaken to satisfy for. It is true, the martyrs that have suffered for Christ, have entertained the greatest torments, and the most terrible deaths, without any such sorrow and consternation; have called their prisons their delectable orchards, and a bed of flames a bed of roses: but then, (1) Christ was now denied the supports and comforts which they had; that is, he denied them to himself, and his soul refused to be comforted, not in passion, but

in justice to his undertaking. Their cheerfulness under the cross was owing to the divine favour, which, for the present, was suspended from the Lord Jesus. (2) his sufferings were of another nature from theirs. St. Paul, when he is to be offered upon the sacrifice and service of the saints' faith, can joy and rejoice with them all; but to be offered a sacrifice, to make atonement for sin, is quite a different case. On the saints' cross there is a blessing pronounced, which enables them to rejoice under it but to Christ's cross there was a curse annexed, which made him sorrowful and very heavy under it." Can you, even now, in your affliction and trial, thank Him for His immeasurable suffering and love for you? Why not spend time doing so?

3. The following verses speak of God's wisdom, faithfulness, and love. As you read and meditate on them, ask God to build steadfastness into your heart. Remember, His wisdom will never lead you where His love wouldn't want you to go and His faithfulness can't keep you: Psalms 33:4; 89:8; 92:1–2; 119:89–90; 142:1–7; Proverbs 8:12, 27–31; Ephesians 3:17–19.

4. Henry Wadsworth Longfellow wrote the following verses about the lighthouse. How does this poem speak to you about God's attributes and what He's making you to be?

> Steadfast, serene, immovable, the same,
> Year after year, through all the silent night
> Burns on forevermore that quenchless flame,
> Shines on that inextinguishable light![10]

5. Summarize what you've learned in four or five sentences.

My Whole Heart Sings!

I will sing and make melody! . . . Awake, O harp and lyre!
(Ps. 67:7, 8 ESV)

From his dismal underground chamber, David got a glimpse of his God. O God! Your steadfast love is great to the heavens! Your faithfulness to the clouds! I will sing and make melody! I will give thanks to you, O Lord, among the peoples; I will sing praises to you among the nations!

You can imagine how out of place such heartfelt worship would have seemed to David's men, in that grim and funereal cavern. In some ways it must have seemed to them as though he was singing praises from his grave. But David's heart, through the grace of God, penetrated a deeper reality. He had grasped the beauty of his God, and he burst out with song and praise. He commands himself to spiritual consciousness: "Awake, my soul!"[1] Where are my instruments? "Awake, O harp and lyre!" Is it too early? "I will awaken the dawn!"

Does this kind of heartfelt, exuberant worship seem out of place to you in your grim and funereal cavern? Does the thought of singing and praising God in this way feel unseemly or hypocritical? I know that there have been times in my life when it would have for me.

In this chapter, I'll not suggest that you break out into a raucous chorus of praise in the midst of a hospital room, but I will encourage you that David and millions of believers through the ages have responded to afflictions and suffering with joyful song. Why? Is it because they are insensible to their circumstance? No, not at all. It's because they're aware of a more profound truth: God's steadfast love and faithfulness is great to the heavens! He will hide them in the shadow of His wings until this temporal destruction passes by. He will fulfill all His purposes! He will send from heaven and save His children! "When God is coming towards us with his favours we must go forth to meet him with our praises."[2] God's people have been "going forth to meet him with our praises" for centuries.

Throughout the epochs of the Old Testament, God's people worshiped Him in the midst of their suffering. From David's dismal cave to Daniel's terrifying den and Shadrack, Meshach, and Abednego's descent into the furnace, believers have worshiped God in the most extraordinary places. But this wasn't only the experience of the saints of old. It's been the constant testimony of all who have come after them, including the founding fathers of the church.

Songs from a Philippian Jail

In response to a vision, pleading with them to "come to Macedonia and help," Paul, Silas, Luke, Timothy, and others traveled to Philippi. After a time of prayer and witnessing at the river's edge, Paul exorcised a spirit of divination from a slave girl. The response of her owners to this miraculous blessing was to have Paul and Silas dragged into the marketplace, falsely accused, stripped, and beaten with rods.

> When they had struck them with many blows, they threw them into prison, commanding the jailer to guard them securely; and he, having received such a command, threw them into the inner prison and fastened their feet in the stocks. (Acts 16:23–24)

I know that this story may be familiar to you, but I'd like to encourage you to read the quote above again. Paul and Silas had been humiliated before the pagan crowd, treated as common criminals, and struck with "many blows." That this action stung Paul severely is witnessed to in his letter to the Thessalonians, where he remembered that he had "suffered and been mistreated in Philippi" (1 Thess. 2:2).

After receiving this appalling treatment, the "troublemakers were hustled to the custody of the city jailer . . . who took seriously his orders to guard them securely. Indifferent to their pain, he neither washed their open wounds nor fed them, but immediately fastened their feet in stocks in the jail's inmost cell."[3]

This is the reality of Paul's and Silas's plight: They had been dragged before the crowds in the marketplace, stripped, beaten "with many blows," and consigned to the inner prison or dungeon, where condemned malefactors spent their last hours. This was no tidy cell with overhead lighting and modern conveniences. It was "dark at noon-day, damp and cold, dirty . . . and in every way offensive."[4] And, as if this were not enough, their feet were secured in stocks so that they could not move about even though they would desire to do so in an effort to relieve their pain.

What would your response have been to that kind of treatment? If I had been Silas, I might have wondered about the wisdom of casting the demon out of the slave girl. I might have questioned whether it was a vision from God that had called us to Macedonia and this miserable city. After all, no great revival had taken place upon our arrival. In fact, the only conversions the team had seen were of women—not men in the synagogue, not leading Gentile males—but women who were holding a prayer meeting by a river. I would have been sorely tempted to wonder whether this was a city God had called me to! But that wasn't Paul's and Silas's response. Their response is astonishing: "about midnight Paul and Silas were praying and singing hymns of praise to God" (Acts 16:25).

Transformed Hearts in the Dead of Night

Within the heart of Paul and Silas, the Spirit of God had drawn a portrait: a portrait of the ineffable beauty of the crucified Christ; a portrait that overcame the humiliation, excruciating pain, and hopelessness of their situation. Prayer was offered. Praises were sung. The wounds on their backs continued to ooze, their senses were assaulted by the offensiveness and degradation of their circumstance, their feet were shackled to the filthy floor, but their hearts were free and on fire. In the middle of the night, when they should have been despairing over their desperate plight or complaining about the unjust treatment they had received, we hear their voices praying and singing praises.

Although we don't know what they prayed, could their prayer have differed much from David's prayer, thousands of years before?

> Be merciful to us, O God, be merciful to us, for in you our soul takes refuge, until this storm of destruction passes by. We cry out to God Most High, to God who will fulfill His purposes for us here, in this city. Lord, we believe that you will send from heaven and save us, we believe that you deliver us from those who have trampled on us. (Ps. 57:1–3, paraphrased)

And as they prayed and cried out to the God in whom they trusted, their hearts were lifted, and they found themselves "singing hymns of praise to God." What may have begun as a prayer for deliverance was soon transformed into praise. How often, as we lay our burdened hearts before our King, do we find that they've miraculously taken flight in joyful song? This has been the experience of the saints throughout all ages. Time and again in Scripture, we find prayer becoming praise, such as in Ephesians 3:14–21, where we find Paul praying for believers and then worshiping God for His grace. Can't you hear Paul's song, as he contemplated the great love of his Savior and the immeasurable grace that works in His people? His heart must have shouted, "To Him be the glory in the church and in Christ Jesus to all generations forever and ever!"

In fact, how could prayer not be followed by praise when we consider, as we must in framing our supplications, that we have such a God: a God who condescends to hear us? He leans down and opens his ear to our cries! This great King, who rules over all the earth, stoops to listen to our faint whimpers and then pours out oceans of His mercy and kindness on us! David said, "I love the Lord, because He hears my voice and my supplications" (Ps. 116:1). Praise is simply the normal response of a heart that's been enraptured by the indescribable kindness of God.

Unlike Esther, who had to wonder whether the ungodly king Ahasuerus would execute or welcome her for daring to approach the throne, we have a king who has extended the scepter of His grace to us and invited us to come boldly to Him (Heb. 4:15–16; 10:19–23). As we consider the great mercy and benevolence of our omnipotent King, won't our hearts be naturally bent to worship and praise? This isn't something we have to work and hope for; this is something that will flow spontaneously from a heart that's been transformed by a God who has visited it with the fire of His Spirit—a heart that's been prepared for it's eternal employments in heaven:

> The saints and angels in heaven in all their perfection are exceedingly affected when they behold and contemplate the perfection of God's works. Their love is as a pure heavenly flame of fire, as is the greatness and strength of their joy and gratitude. Their praises are represented as the voice of many waters and as the voice of a great thunder. *For they respond perfectly to the greatness of God's love.*[5]

"Glad and devoted and reverent worship is," A. W. Tozer writes, "the normal employment of moral beings."[6] Have you experienced the wonderful transformation that occurs when your heart has been lifted to your Father in humble supplication? Even in the darkest cell, in the deepest pit, His Spirit can warm and transform your heart from wintry unbelief to radiant, exuberant faith that breaks out into worshipful song. Is it the dead of night for your soul? Do you feel as though your heart's been beaten? Have you been humiliated by the ungodly, accused falsely, or shackled to a dank prison wall? Let the wings your heart take flight as you offer your prayer to the God of the heavens and sing praises to the one who is worthy!

The Song of the Lamb

What were they singing that night, so many years ago? Were they singing one of the psalms they had memorized or perhaps a hymn about the risen Christ? Perhaps they were singing like David before them, "Our hearts are steadfast, O God, our hearts are steadfast! We will sing and make melody . . . for your steadfast love is great to the heavens, your faithfulness to the clouds!" (Ps. 57:7, 10, paraphrased from ESV).

We don't know exactly what they sang, but we do know that their hearts were so lifted in praise that their neighbors heard them. "But about midnight Paul and Silas were praying and singing hymns of praise to God, and the prisoners were listening to them" (Acts 16:25).

I can imagine that "hymns of praise to God" was not what was commonly voiced in that miserable prison. Surely there were prayers offered to different gods or to any god that might hear, but hymns of praise? Who would praise any god for a cell in that wretched prison? Who would give thanks and praise for a chance to "suffer for His name"? Who indeed. The praise that has resonated from the hearts of believers who have lived through trial, affliction, persecution, and spirit-crushing pain distinguishes them from sufferers in the world who scream out for comfort, relief, deliverance, and justice.

This song of praise is going to be our eternal employment in the concert hall of heaven. When the Spirit opened the celestial doors to John the Revelator, what did John see? He saw living creatures and elders and "the voice of many angels, numbering myriads of myriads and thousands of thousands, saying with a loud voice, 'Worthy is the Lamb who was slain, to receive power and wealth and wisdom and might and honor and glory and blessing!' " (Rev. 5:11–12 ESV). The worship that fills heaven is centered on the Lamb who was slain to purchase our souls for God. It is the same for us now. When we lift our eyes to behold Him, to see His cross and His marvelous love, worship and adoration for this great love naturally springs forth from our redeemed hearts.

The Grace to Praise Him

I know that you would not have picked up this book or stayed with me for so long if you weren't going through a storm of your own. I know that you may feel as though, like David, your "soul is in the midst of lions." I can also imagine that some of you may want to praise your Savior, but your heart isn't in it. You might be thinking, *To praise God in this circumstance, with the way that I'm feeling would be hypocritical. I can't thank Him for this—I'm having enough trouble believing that He's even here.* If you resonate with that sentiment, please let me encourage you in two ways.

First, let me encourage you that although it is right to have joyous affections when praising God, he understands your frame. He knows that you are "but dust" (Ps. 103:14). He understands your heart, your desire to love and please Him, and the circumstance that's threatening to engulf you. He's not looking for perfection in word or heart from you. That perfection has already been supplied by His Son. Because He loves and knows you so well, and because He wants you to address yourself to Him, you might pray to Him in this way.

> *Father, I know that you have commanded me to worship you in gladness with my whole heart, but I confess that I am struggling with your righteous command. I do not want to be false with You, for You see my heart and know me perfectly, and so I ask for your forgiveness for the coldness of my heart. Even though I recognize my sin, I also believe that the perfect record of the worship of Your Son is mine and that you hear me because of Him. Father, I ask that your grace would envelope my heart and that your Spirit would come to me and make your kindnesses and graces precious to me, so that I can worship you as you deserve to be worshiped. I come to you in the name of your holy Son, whose heart was always attuned to your praise and in whose record I stand. Amen.*

In praying in this way, you are asking Him to make your heart into what it should be, filled with praise.

If you're having trouble believing that He is even here, listening to you, please take time to soak yourself in the refreshing water of the truth. Below I've supplied some verses on God's presence and ability to hear your cry. Please ask Him to use them to renew a heart of praise.

> I love You, O Lord, my strength. The Lord is my rock and my fortress and my deliverer, My God, my rock, in whom I take refuge; My shield and the horn of my salvation, my stronghold. I call upon the Lord, who is worthy to be praised, and I am saved from my enemies. (Ps. 18:1–3)

Behold, God is my helper; the LORD is the sustainer of my soul. . . . Willingly I will sacrifice to You; I will give thanks to Your name, O LORD, for it is good. (Ps. 54:4, 6)

For You have been my help, and in the shadow of Your wings I sing for joy. My soul clings to You; Your right hand upholds me. (Ps. 63:7–8)

If the LORD had not been my help, my soul would soon have dwelt in the abode of silence. If I should say, "My foot has slipped," Your lovingkindness, O LORD, will hold me up. When my anxious thoughts multiply within me, Your consolations delight my soul. . . . But the LORD has been my stronghold, and my God the rock of my refuge. (Ps. 94:17–18, 22)

As Charles Spurgeon said, "There is no place to which you can be banished where God is not near, and there is no time of day or night when His throne is inaccessible. The caves have heard the best prayers. Some of God's people shine brightest in the dark."[7]

The Prisoners Aren't the Only Ones Listening

Let's visit Paul and Silas one more time in their dungeon. The narrative continues, "But about midnight Paul and Silas were praying and singing hymns of praise to God, and the prisoners were listening to them; and suddenly there came a great earthquake, so that the foundations of the prison house were shaken; and immediately all the doors were opened and everyone's chains were unfastened" (Acts 16:25–26). The prisoners heard Paul's and Silas's songs and prayer, but they weren't the only ones. The Lord Himself heard their prayer and responded to it in a miraculous way. Their chains were loosed. The doors to every cell were opened. This outcome was probably as astonishing to Paul and Silas as it is to us.

We need to realize that God worked sovereignly in the lives of the early apostles, in ways that were unusual. He was doing so because He was establishing His church and was glorifying His Son, proving His deity. In this circumstance, the Lord's good will was to release many people, both body and soul. In other cases, it's His will to allow His children to suffer "chains and imprisonment" (Heb. 11:36). Because we are not all-wise or omniscient, none of us knows what the future might hold for us or our loved ones. What we do know, though, is that God is good and that He will release you and me from our prison of affliction when it is best. Of this, we can be certain.[8]

Release from a Different Kind of Prison

Whether it is God's will to calm your storm or to add another dimension to it, we don't know. What we can be sure of, though, is that when we approach our gracious King with prayer and praise, we'll be freed from our prison house of fears and terrors, and we'll know the guarding power of the Holy Spirit, as Paul reminded the Philippians.

Rejoice in the Lord always; again I will say, rejoice! Let your gentle spirit be known to all men. The Lord is near. Be anxious for nothing, but in everything by prayer and supplication with thanksgiving let your requests be made known to God. And the peace of God, which surpasses all comprehension, will guard your hearts and your minds in Christ Jesus. (Phil. 4:4–7)

Paul knew what it was to rejoice in the Lord, didn't he? He knew that His Lord was near and that He heard his thankful supplication. The Philippians knew it, too, because they had seen the reality of it in Paul and heard about it from the Philippian jailer and probably other prisoners who had been awakened at midnight by a strange but winsome sound.

> When Paul wrote from another prison, urging the Philippians to join his rejoicing in his sufferings for their faith, those who remembered that strange hymn singing at midnight could attest to his joy in adverse circumstances (Phil. 1:12, 18, 29–30; 2:17–18). When adversity dampens our mood, we need to sink the roots of our joy more deeply into the Lord himself, rather than relying on surface circumstances (Phil. 4:4).[9]

What is Paul's counsel to those who find themselves beaten, falsely accused, in pain, and shackled to what seems like a hopeless and endless imprisonment of affliction? "Rejoice!" Twice Paul enjoins the suffering, "Rejoice!"

Rejoice? How Can I Do That?

You might be wondering, *How am I supposed to do that?* How gracious is the Holy Spirit, who not only informs us of God's commands but also tells us what we need to know to obey them! How are we to rejoice?

We are to remember that the Lord is near. The nearness of our God is one of the most precious gifts we have. We're not alone—whether we're in a dungeon of despair or hiding in a cave, the Lord is near. Therefore we can "confidently say, 'the Lord is my helper! I will not be afraid!' " (Heb. 13:6).

We are to bring our desires to our King. Paul does not tell us to ignore our problems or rise above them. He counsels us to bring our cares to the Father because He cares for us. We can supplicate and intercede, we can confess and implore. God's ear is open and He loves to hear and answer us. Have you prayed already? I know you have. Our Savior instructs us that we must continue to pray, even when our prayers have seemingly gone unanswered for years.

Jesus told a parable about an unjust judge who did not fear God or respect man. To this wicked judge a defenseless widow kept coming, asking for legal protection. The judge, who didn't care one whit about the widow, eventually answered her prayer because of her persistence. He finishes His story with these words, "And the Lord said, '. . . will not God bring about justice for His elect who cry to Him day and night, and will He delay long over them? I tell you that He will bring about justice for them quickly' " (Luke 18:6–8a).

Our Savior is bringing encouragement to you now: continue on in prayer "at all times," "day and night," and don't give in to discouragement. We know that our God hears us; that He loves us, and that He will answer us quickly.[10]

God isn't purposely slow, drawing out our afflictions because He's busy elsewhere or unconcerned. He will answer us in haste. This affliction will not last one instant longer than is good for you and glorifying to Him. He loves you and carries your afflictions in His own heart.[11] At this point it might also be helpful to remember that "with the Lord one day is like a thousand years, and a thousand years like one day." Even so, "The Lord is not slow about His promise . . . but is patient toward you, not wishing for any to perish but for all to come to repentance" (2 Peter 3:8–9). Just as Paul and Silas didn't know that the spread of the gospel was to spring forth from their imprisonment, you and I don't know how He will use our storms. Your prayer in affliction or praise in suffering might be the means that God will use to set captives free.

We are to bring praise and thanksgiving to our King. Paul tells us, "Follow me as I follow Christ." Whether we're in a prison cell, a bleak cave, a hospital bed, or a shadowy cave filled with the specters of grief to come, we're to pray with thanksgiving.

Your Personal Thanksgiving

What are you thankful for? If you're having trouble thinking of anything, why not start with the basics? Are you thankful for the incarnation? That God became man to offer you salvation should be a comforting source of thanks. Are you thankful for the Lord's perfect life? That He fulfilled every law for your sake, so that He might be a perfect sacrifice in your place, is wondrous, indeed. Are you thankful that He suffered humiliation, pain, separation from His Father, and God's just wrath so that you can now have peace with Him? Have you remembered your spiritual adoption? Are you thankful that you can now cry to Him and address Him as "Abba," your loving Father? I trust that these thoughts are beginning to warm you to the idea of thanksgiving.

Perhaps you don't feel as though you can thank Him for your circumstance yet. Why not begin here: Thank Him for the circumstances He endured for the sake of your eternal joy and then ask Him for the grace to see that everything in your life is meant to eventuate in your eternal happiness.

Puritan Richard Baxter once wrote, "He will use us only for safe and honorable purposes and to no worse end than our endless happiness."[12] What has he done to obtain your endless happiness? Perhaps you aren't feeling very happy right now, but rest, dear sister, in this truth, happiness is coming and nothing can stop it.

The peace of God will guard your heart and mind. The Spirit's promise to those who bring their petitions to the throne and then linger there in grateful praise: Peace; God's peace that will act as a guard over your heart and mind. He'll keep you from terror and despair. He'll give you His peace that will act as a sentinel at the gates of your heart!

The Shadow of Death

Close by my house there are delightful walking trails through undeveloped brush land, where it is my habit and joy to walk with my grandchildren. From time to time as we amble through these hills, we'll hear a mysterious sound in a nearby shrub. Sometimes that sound can be a little spooky: *Wonder what that is?* we say. *Is it a snake or a robber?* We giggle and run down the trail.

During the final weeks of our latest affliction, when everything seemed to be getting bleaker and more hopeless, the Lord spoke into my heart a sweet truth about these little walks. It was important for me, I learned, while I was walking on this shadowy path of affliction, to keep my eyes on the trail right in front of me. It was foolish and only added to my fear for me to stare off under bushes and behind fallen logs. What might be lurking there was not to be my immediate concern. I understood that some of what I was suffering was because I kept trying to peer under every rock to see what scary thing might possibly pop out at me next. At this point my imagination was my own worst enemy. Instead of peering into obscure shadows and worst-case scenarios, I should have been gazing at the compassionate face of my Savior and rejoicing in what He had accomplished for my soul.

What shadows are frightening you today? Are they real troubles facing you, or are they merely terrifying figments of an imagination that's pondered the inside of a cave too long? How long has it been since you've sung the song of the Lamb? How long since you've asked Him to clear your mind of spectral shadows in the valley of the shadow of death and asked for a picture of the love demonstrated on Calvary or the power of the empty tomb instead? When I'm captivated by those images, my heart naturally bursts forth in confident and joyful song.

As you work through the questions below, ask Him to help you keep your eyes focused on the path beneath your feet, using His word as your lamp and His Spirit as guide.

Finding His Comfort in the Midst of the Storm

1. David and Paul found the secret of God's comfort in the storm: keeping their heart focused on prayer and praise. Why not write out a prayer that is laced with much praise now and ask the Lord to once again warm your affections to Him?

2. If you're still struggling to bring your heart into line, refer again to the verses on pp. 129–30. You might also consider the following verses: Psalms 118:7–9; 124:8; Romans 8:31.

3. Noted twentieth-century author and pastor A. W. Tozer wrote, "Jesus was born of a virgin, suffered under Pontius Pilate, died on the cross and rose from the

grave to make worshipers out of rebels!"[13] What do you think God is doing in your life through this trial? Is He seeking to make you a worshiper? Why or why not?

4. The prayer and praise of Paul and Silas taught the inmates of the Philippian jail about their God. Paul wrote to the church at Colossae, "Let the word of Christ richly dwell within you, with all wisdom teaching and admonishing one another with psalms and hymns and spiritual songs, singing with thankfulness in your hearts to God" (Col. 3:16). Who are you teaching and admonishing by your praise?

5. For further encouragement to prayer and praise, you might consider the following verses: "I called on Your name, O LORD, out of the lowest pit. You have heard my voice; Do not hide Your ear from my prayer for relief, from my cry for help. You drew near when I called on You; You said, 'Do not fear!' " (Lam. 3:55–57). See also Psalm 77:6–14; Isaiah 30:29; 2 Corinthians 6:10; Philippians 2:17; 1Thessalonians 5:16–18.

6. Listen again to the music on the CD that was included with this book. The lyrics are on pp. 13–14. Why not sing along with Vikki and ask the Lord to fill your heart with song?

7. Summarize what you've learned in this chapter in four or five sentences.

Be Exalted, O God!

*Be exalted, O God, above the heavens! Let your glory be over
all the earth! (Ps. 57:5 ESV)*

As we've moved through our psalm together, we've seen a
transformation in David's heart, haven't we? Where he
once prayed about "storms of destruction" and "fiery beasts,"
now his heart is filled with song and he wants to let God's
praises ring out among the nations. Let's remember that this
transformation didn't happen because David's circumstances
had changed. This transformation occurred because the Spirit
had inclined his heart to focus on a different reality. In the end,
he was focused on the glory and exaltation of God.

Joining David in the cave and Paul in the prison cell is
another man, bereft of his enormous wealth, his beloved family, his good reputation, and his health. Once elevated as a wise

ruler at the city gates, he now makes his home atop an ash heap, scraping his painful sores with a piece of broken pottery. His friends mercilessly accuse him of malfeasance, while his wife with broken heart admonishes him to give up his integrity and turn his back on his God. This man who is synonymous with affliction is Job, to whom we will now turn our attention, as we close our time together.

The Misery of Job

When the Holy Spirit began His narrative of a particular season in the life of this Old Testament saint, Job is described as "the greatest of all the people of the east" (Job 1:3 ESV). Not only was Job wealthy in progeny, lands, and livestock, but also he is described as a man who was "blameless and upright, one who feared God and turned away from evil" (Job 1:1 ESV). Job's righteousness and scruples about his religious practices were well known. He "continually" offered burnt offerings for his family, lest they might have turned their backs on God and sinned. Job's life was impeccable: he treasured God's words more than food (Job 23:11–12); wasn't aware of any inner secret sins (Job 31:33); was a respected judge in the community (Job 29:7–8); didn't abuse his power (Job 29:15); maintained moral purity (Job 31:1, 5, 7); and didn't put his confidence in his great wealth (Job 31:24–25).

God directs Satan's attention to Job and testifies of him, "there is none like him on the earth." Of course Satan hated Job; he stood for everything Satan despised—a life lived for the glory of the God he hated. And so he makes his accusation: "Does Job fear God for no reason?" In essence he charged God with being less than the most delightful being in all the earth and said, "You protect him and prosper him! Of course he loves you! He doesn't love you because you're so worthy of love. He loves you because you pay him well! If you take away what he has, he'll curse you to your face!" Satan throws down the gauntlet at the feet of the almighty King, and God, for His glory and Job's good (although Satan surely didn't know that!), allowed the devil to afflict him.

Job's fall from influence and prosperity is so great, it's almost impossible to imagine. On one day he lost all his wealth: eleven thousand animals and the servants who were guarding them were struck by raiders or by fire falling from heaven. While Job was receiving these reports, an even more grievous one reached his ear.

> Your sons and daughters were eating and drinking wine in their oldest brother's house, and behold, a great wind came across the wilderness and struck the four corners of the house, and it fell upon the young people, and they are dead, and I alone have escaped to tell you.(Job 1:18–19 ESV)

At this news, Job's faith burst into a white-hot flame, and he spoke those celebrated and precious words: "The LORD gave, and the LORD has taken away; blessed be the name of the LORD" (Job 1:21 ESV). In this, the beginning of his time of suffering, Job didn't sin or "charge God with wrong." But this wasn't the end of his suffering; his suffering had only just begun.

At some later date, in emerging horror, Job began to sense an excruciating pain spreading throughout his whole body and breaking out in "loathsome sores from the sole of his foot to the crown of his head" (Job 2:7 ESV). The exact nature of these offensive and painful ulcers, which covered his entire body, are unknown to us, but the Bible gives us enough information to get a glimpse into his suffering: he had "inflamed eruptions (Job 2:7); maggots in the ulcers (Job 7:5); terrifying dreams (Job 7:14); running tears blinding the eyes (Job 16:16); fetid breath (Job 19:17); emaciated body (Job 19:20); erosion of the bones (Job 30:17); blackening and peeling off of the skin (Job 30:30)."[1]

As if all this—the loss of family, prosperity, and health, the unkind and heartless counsel of his friends, and the broken-hearted and faltering admonitions of his wife weren't enough—the struggle that most overwhelmed Job's soul and tortured his faithful heart was his inability to reconcile his present circumstances with what he believed about God's goodness and his own character. Job was in great turmoil and distress, but his greatest distress didn't originate from without. It came, rather, from within, from a faith that had been shredded by circumstances and accusations so vile that he didn't know if anything he had believed remained sure. Although his faith was strong and good, it was not yet fully mature. Job needed to experience firsthand the astounding truth that God's love is so deep that He's willing to ordain what He hates (Satan's cruel activity) to accomplish what He loves (the blessing of Job and the ultimate demonstration of His glory). Job needed a more comprehensive understanding of the depth of God's love: a love that will bless integrity, certainly, but also a love that will strip and afflict as blessing. This intense commitment to the ultimate happiness of Job's soul proceeded from the God who loved and delighted in his blamelessness and integrity, who bragged about him to His enemy, and who ultimately loved him enough to chastise him for giving voice to his doubts about whether He was really perfectly wise, powerful, and loving. Job's greatest pains were the growing pains of his faith, although he didn't know it yet.

Job believed in an absolute and overarching sovereignty . . . but that was the rub: since God was, as he believed, in complete control of everything, why would he afflict his righteous soul? This is the precious truth that the book brings to us: God is absolutely sovereign. He does reward faithful obedience with blessings as Job believed, but He also brings blessings in the form of afflictions so that Job and all believers may more fully grasp His nature and in particular, the vast compassion God has for a human soul and ultimately for His own glory.

The Differing Levels of Your Tears

Perhaps you've discovered, as Job did, that your affliction has layers. There are the presenting afflictions: the trial as it has first come to you, whether that's homelessness after a natural disaster, the loss of a loved one or a beloved relationship, an ongoing wasting disease, difficulty at home or work, or whatever affliction you're currently facing. Then there's the underlying problem: the questions, the doubts and uncertainty about God and your relationship to Him. Is God angry? Is He punishing you? Is there a direct one-for-one correlation between your sin and His providence? Does He hate you? Is He evil? Do your feeble and flawed efforts to remain faithful displease Him?

The book of Job is meant, in part, to answer these questions. It's meant to tell you that affliction doesn't mean His displeasure—in Job's case the truth was the opposite, wasn't it? The book is also meant to tell you what glorifying Him in trial looks like—and because Job stands as our example, we can rest in the comforting thought that God knows our capacities, knows what His Spirit will accomplish, and is confident that we'll bring Him glory at the end. Job comes through his trial and proves Satan's charges false, but he doesn't come through it sinlessly. He wrestles with God, and he does stumble, but the faith that God had planted in his heart remains true.

In His wisdom God wanted Job to see that it was His mercy that brought him misery, so that he might have a more perfect understanding of the one who is the fountain of all delights. God was giving Job the most wonderful gift anyone could give: a better understanding of Himself.

Job's Heart Is Transformed

Just as David had a turning point when he stopped focusing on his afflictions and began to see the greatness of his God, so did Job. Up until Job 19, Job's complaint and misery is almost completely hopeless and despairing.[2] He wonders why he was ever born and why light is "given to him who is in misery, and life to the bitter in soul, who long for death, but it comes not" (Job 3:20–21 ESV). He prays that God would decimate him: "Oh that I might have my request, and that God would fulfill my hope, that it would please God to crush me" (Job 6:8–9 ESV). He wonders whether the just God he's always loved is unjust (Job 9:22–24). Job's speech is filled with the same sentiments that David expressed, "My soul is in the midst of lions, I lie down amid fiery beasts" (Ps. 57:4 ESV).

And then, miraculously, the Spirit brings Job revelation of someone who will rescue him from his despair. Job realizes that God is not his enemy and cries out,

142

For I know that my Redeemer lives, and at the last he will stand upon the earth. And after my skin has been thus destroyed, yet in my flesh I shall see God, whom I shall see for myself, and my eyes shall behold, and not another. (Job 19:25–27 ESV)

Job is not exulting because he believes his trial to be ending. He is rejoicing because he now believes, by the Spirit, that he has a Redeemer, a heavenly kinsman who will come to his aid. The role of the kinsman-redeemer was well known in the ancient Near East, and it is to this Job is referring. The next of kin was to "redeem his [relative's] property, and restore it to him if he had in any way forfeited it or been obliged to sell it; to defend him against injury and wrong; and, especially, to avenge his blood if he had been unrighteously slain."[3]

Job now sees God as his Kinsman-Redeemer, and although he is convinced that he will shortly die from his disease, he confidently announces that even after his skin has been destroyed, he will in his flesh see God! In Job's sorely tried heart, God is no longer the enemy who is pursuing him unjustly; he is now his friend who will sustain him in eternity.

In his own esteem he is sinking into the grave with every indication surrounding him of God's relentless hostility; every possibility of a return of God's favour to him in this life is, to his mind, utterly shut out; and *yet so fixed is he in his inward persuasion of the real friendship and redeeming grace of God to him, that he bursts the boundaries of time, passes the limits of the visible and the tangible, and knows that the manifest tokens of the divine love, which are denied him here, will be granted to him there.*[4]

Our Blessed Redeemer

Job was unaware of our New Covenant understanding of the Redeemer, and yet the truth that there is someone who has come to our aid, vile, blind, and spiritually dead on the ash heap of sin as we are, was just as precious to him as it is to us. We've seen what this Redeemer looks like. We've studied His words and observed His life. We know that our Redeemer lives and that we will behold Him one day! Paul writes of Him,

> But when the fullness of the time came, God sent forth His Son, born of a woman, born under the Law, so that He might redeem those who were under the Law, that we might receive the adoption as sons. Because you are sons, God has sent forth the Spirit of His Son into our hearts, crying, "Abba! Father!" Therefore you are no longer a slave, but a son; and if a son, then an heir through God. (Gal. 4:4–7)

This is the truth that Job and all believers who suffer need to hear: God has sent forth His Redeemer to bring us adoption. We are no longer strangers or slaves, hoping that we don't offend a harsh and demanding taskmaster. God has committed Himself to us and has welcomed us into His family as His beloved children. Our Redeemer perfectly passed every test the enemy could assail Him with: He lived a sinless life, He refused Satan's most malicious machinations, and even as His holy heart was trembling before the measureless wrath of God, He perfectly submitted Himself to the will of His Father. We can be confidently assured of this: Because of His substitutionary atonement, the record of every failure and unwillingness to submit to suffering and our Father's will is obliterated and our history is now one of gentle humility, cheerful obedience, and patient faithfulness in the jaws of every odious affliction. We can cry to Him "Abba! Father!" and we can know that we are heard and that God looks at our lives and reports, "Here is a blameless and upright woman who fears God and turns away from evil!"

You have a Redeemer who lives and who will one day stand upon the earth. Even when your flesh has been destroyed and turned back into the dust from which it came, you will with your eyes see Him. Take courage from these truths, dear sister. God is not your enemy, slave master, or evil tyrant—He's your Redeemer. You can trust Him and rest in His strong embrace.

Truth from a Transformed Heart

From this point on, the tenor of Job's complaint is changed. That's not to say that he no longer struggled or sought to ascertain why the wicked prosper; it's just that the deep despair and bitterness is gone from him. Soon, he'll receive the wise counsel of Elihu, who will prepare the way for the astounding counsel of the Lord. His heart has been prepared: Job is about to receive the most precious treasure ever imagined. At the end of his trial, Job describes his new treasure in few but powerful phrases:

> I know that You can do all things, and that no purpose of Yours can be thwarted. . . . I have declared that which I did not understand, things too wonderful for me, which I did not know. . . . I have heard of You by the hearing of the ear; but now my eye sees You. . . . (Job 42:2–3, 5)

"Now my eye sees You," is Job's final speech. What was God's gracious plan for Job? That he would see Him as He really is—not as some celestial vending machine who dispenses good for good and evil for evil. He's come to see God, and in the process, he's seen himself. If there was self-righteousness and pride in him, Job was now fully aware of it: "I despise myself, and repent in dust and ashes," he confesses (Job 42:6 ESV).

The final state of Job is the repudiation of all that Satan had proposed: that Job loved God and walked in integrity only because God bribed him to do so. It is the final refutation of all his contemptible lies: that God hates you, that He is afflicting you because He is unjust, that your faith is a sham. The resounding reply flies from the faithful heart of Job and shatters all of Satan's vile assertions: the true knowledge of the Creator humbles all created beings and places them in the dust (where the serpent belonged) before Him. God is faithful and will be faithful to redeem and rescue His own. All other creatures must bow in subjection before this mighty King. Satan is vanquished. Job is properly humbled, instructed, and comforted by God's sustaining grace, and in the end (was there ever any doubt?) God is glorified.

Job's Steadfast Heart

In encouraging the persecuted church of the Dispersion to persevere in severe affliction, James reminds us again of our dear brother, Job: "Behold, we consider those blessed who remained steadfast. You have heard of the steadfastness of Job, and you have seen the purpose of the Lord, how the Lord is compassionate and merciful" (James 5:11 ESV).

What was God's purpose in Job's trial? It was to silence lying Worm Tongue, but that wasn't God's only purpose. His purpose was to open Job's eyes to who He is, a God who is compassionate and merciful, and to sustain within him a steadfastness that would be spoken of for millennia to come. You've heard of the steadfastness of Job—and you don't know who has heard of your steadfastness—but your steadfastness does prove one thing: Your God is compassionate and merciful.

Do you know that your Redeemer lives? I trust that you do. Do you want to exalt Him and see His glory over all the earth? Of course you do. He knows this, loves you, and will see that your life decimates your enemy's lies and brings Him great joy, when on that last day you stand on the earth with your near Kinsman and gaze upon His beautiful, compassionate, and merciful face.

How Will He Glorify Himself?

In our time of trial, Phil and I didn't know what would best glorify Him, and I'll suppose it's the same for you. On one hand, we knew that it might glorify Him to allow us to be stripped of all our possessions. The way that we knew He would sustain us even in deprivation, would, we trusted, bring Him great glory. It would glorify Him as people who knew us could see that His grace was strong enough to maintain our souls, even if we lost all our earthly possessions.

On the other hand, there was a possibility that God might deliver us—in some mysterious way that none of us could fathom. That, too, we knew, could bring Him glory and cause people to rejoice in His goodness. We wanted to be careful not to assume that we could divine the future—or even create it by our prayers or good confession. We knew we should pray, "Glorify yourself and build your kingdom. Let your will be done, here in our lives and by us, just as it's done in heaven!"

I don't want to give you an undeserved good impression of my response to our trial, as if I never struggled or doubted or questioned God's wisdom and love. I'll honestly admit that there were days when I forgot the "glorify yourself" and only meditated on the evil that I felt others were perpetrating upon us. There were days filled with *if onlys . . .* and *why didn't you? . . .* and *How dare they?* It was particularly on those days when God would "send from heaven and save me," primarily by reminding me that my life and my possessions didn't belong to me anyway and that I am here to bring Him pleasure (Ps. 149:4). *Oh yes, Lord, now I remember: Be exalted, O God . . . however you might do this! Please help me remain humble and faithful, no matter what happens!*

On those days, when my heart had been corrected by His kind condescension from heaven, I would stand steadfast in faith and in my determination to praise Him, come what may. Although there usually weren't any significant outward changes to our circumstances (at least not for the better!), there were important inward changes in my heart. Did I still feel the storm of destruction? Yes. Was my soul in the midst of fiery beasts who were seeking to destroy it? Still yes. But my perspective on my persecutors' ability to harm us and the outcome of their schemes was transformed. Had they "dug a pit in my way"? Yes, but they wouldn't be ultimately successful in ensnaring our souls.

In the same way that I didn't know what God's glory would look like in my own life, I can't tell you what it will look like in yours. Will He heal you or allow you to undergo pain and ultimately death? Will He change your loved one's heart or will He allow him to continue on without any glimmer of alteration? Will He answer your prayer for a spouse or a child or will He sustain you in your singleness and seeming emptiness? Will

He transform the heart of your employer or will he grow more and more demanding and vile? I don't know, and I don't believe that the Bible teaches us that we can command God to glorify Himself by acquiescing to our will. In this, as in all things, we must embrace the superiority of His wisdom and say, "*Lord, you alone know best how to glorify yourself. Please do so.*"

It's that prayer and the confident knowledge that He will always glorify Himself that can bring to us great courage and consolation. But in praying that God would glorify Himself, we can also be sure that we aren't praying against our own best interests. We are praying for them. *God, we pray, glorify yourself, and we know that in doing so, you'll also accomplish our greatest good.* John Calvin wrote that it is no "small comfort to consider that God, in appearing for the help of His people, at the same time advances His own glory."[5]

The Purpose of the Lord

David, Job, Daniel, and even our great Savior, Jesus, have each been memorialized in Scripture that we might have hope (Rom. 15:4) and that we might know more of God's character: that He is compassionate and merciful (James 5:11). It is with this perspective that we draw our discussion about His comforting presence in our storm to a close. We can have hope—hope that this trial is for our good, will result in His glory, and will one day end. We can know Him, that He is filled with compassion and mercy for us, and that He will not allow this affliction to continue on one second longer than is necessary for our good.

The writers of the Heidelberg Catechism formulated this comforting answer to the question that we all ask, especially during our times of trial: "What is thy only comfort in life and death?" The answer below is meant to sustain, encourage, and comfort you as you walk step by step on this sometimes dimly lit path where, like Job, we're blindfolded in the darkness of divine providence but trusting that our Redeemer lives:

> That I with body and soul, both in life and death, am not my own, but belong unto my faithful Saviour Jesus Christ; who, with his precious blood, has fully satisfied for all my sins, and delivered me from all the power of the devil; and so preserves me that without the will of my heavenly Father, not a hair can fall from my head; yea, that all things must be subservient to my salvation, and therefore, by his Holy Spirit, He also assures me of eternal life, and makes me sincerely willing and ready, henceforth, to live unto him.

The Sole Source of Your Comfort

Let me encourage you to drink deeply of the truth found in this catechism question and answer. What is your only comfort in life and in death? Although I've tried by God's grace to bring you comfort through this book, I can't comfort you the way you need to be comforted. The only thought that will bring you the comfort you're seeking in your affliction is this: you belong to your faithful Savior, Jesus Christ. He is so jealous over you and carefully watching over every aspect of your life that "without the will of your heavenly Father, not a hair can fall from [your] head!" In fact His love is so great that everything that intersects with your life, whether blessing or trial, must serve the greater goal of your salvation and your glorifying of Him. Of this you can rest assured: He is being exalted in you, and you will bring Him glory!

Finding God's Comfort in the Midst of Your Storm

1. God's glorifying Himself results in people and supernatural beings being amazed at His character. How do you think the Lord is glorifying Himself through your difficulties? Have you been guilty of assuming that you knew how He would best magnify Himself in your trial? If so, why not take time to humbly confess your lack of trust in His wisdom and commit yourself to steadfastly seeking to remember His steadfastness and faithfulness?

2. How does the thought that Christ is your Redeemer encourage and comfort you? Can you sing with Job, "I know that my Redeemer lives?" Read Titus 2:11–14 and ask the Lord to again grant you the joy of your salvation: He gave Himself for your soul, and there's no doubt that you'll make it through to the end.

3. In the past, what did you think "glorifying" God looked like? What did it look like in David's life? Job's life? Although these men were righteous and godly, their responses to their afflictions were not perfect. Yours won't be either. What would it look like for you to glorify God today? Would it mean turning your heart in trust to your Redeemer? Would it mean hanging onto the last vestige of your faith and asking for the Spirit to give you the grace to say, "Be exalted, O God, above the heavens! Let your glory be over all the earth," whatever that means today?

4. Summarize what you've learned from this chapter in three or four sentences.

5. Imagine that your best friend is looking for a book on affliction and wants to know what this book is about. How would you answer her? What did you find helpful? In what ways did you experience the comfort of the Lord as you read it? How have you changed?

Notes

Introduction

1. Hebrews 12:11 (ESV): "For the moment all discipline seems painful rather than pleasant, but later it yields the peaceful fruit of righteousness to those who have been trained by it."

Chapter 1: Our Cry in the Storm

1. Matthew Henry, *Matthew Henry's Commentary on the Whole Bible* (Peabody, Mass.: Hendrickson, 1991), in Biblesoft, *PC Study Bible*, v. 4.2 (Seattle: Biblesoft, 1988–2004).

2. D. R. W. Wood and I. Howard Marshall, *New Bible Dictionary,* 3rd ed. (Downers Grove, Ill.: InterVarsity Press, 1996).

3. *Psalter Hymnal* (Grand Rapids: Publication Committee of the Christian Reformed Church, 1959), doctrinal standards, 22.

Chapter 2: His Forsaken Son

1. Luke 24:27. All of Scripture speaks of Jesus Christ—the psalms most particularly.

2. F. W. Krummacher, *The Suffering Saviour* (Carlisle, Pa.: Banner of Truth Trust, 2004), 384.

3. Ibid., 390–91.

4. W. E. Vine, *Vine's Expository Dictionary of Biblical Words*, Merrill F. Unger, William White, ed., (Nashville: Thomas Nelson, 1985), in Biblesoft, *PC Study Bible*, v. 4.2, (Seattle: Biblesoft, 1988-2004).

5. Ibid.

6. This is the plain teaching of Scripture. If you're His now, you will be His eternally. Of course, this doesn't mean that we should choose to sin capriciously. Those who are truly His won't make a practice of willful sin but will fight against their sin and plead for hatred of it.

7. Adam Clarke, *Clarke's Commentary (1762-1832)* (Nashville: Abingdon Press) in Biblesoft, *PC Study Bible*, v. 4.2 (Seattle: Biblesoft, 1988–2004), Electronic Database, copyright 1996, 2003 by Biblesoft, Inc.

Chapter 3: His Suffering Saints

1. Quote from advertising for *Your Best Life Now* by Joel Osteen, found on Family Christian Stores website of the best-selling books for the week ending June 25, 2005. The author has not read this book and is making no comment on it.

2. Dorothy L. Sayers, *Creed or Chaos? Why Christians Must Choose Either Dogma or Disaster (Or, Why It Really Does Matter What You Believe)* (Manchester, N.H.: Sophia Institute Press, 1974), 60.

3. Jeremiah Burroughs, *The Rare Jewel of Christian Contentment* (Carlisle, Pa.: Banner of Truth Trust, 1995), 37–38.

4. Faith Cook, *Grace in Winter: Rutherford in Verse* (Carlisle, Pa.: Banner of Truth Trust, 1989), 29.

5. Ibid., 37.

6. Carmichael, Amy, "The Abandoned Life," www.intouch.org/myintouch/mighty/portraits/amycarmichael_213673.html.

7. Amy Carmichael, "No Scar," *Toward Jerusalem* (Fort Washington, PA: Christian Literature Crusade, 1977), 85.

8. Distilled from the thought in Joni Eareckson Tada and Steve Estes, *When God Weeps: Why Our Sufferings Matter to the Almighty* (Grand Rapids: Zondervan, 2000), 57–58.

9. Joni Eareckson Tada, *O Worship the King: Hymns of Praise and Assurance to Encourage the Heart* (Wheaton, Ill.: Crossway Books, 2000), 58.

10. Communist exploitation of religion hearing before the subcommittee to investigate the administration of the internal security act and other internal

security laws of the committee on the judiciary; United States Senate, eighty-ninth Congress, second session, testimony of the Rev. Richard Wurmbrand, communist exploitation of religion, Friday, May 6, 1966.

11. Cook, *Grace in Winter,* 37.

Chapter 4: He Comforts His Children

1. Or *checed.*

2. W. E. Vine, *Vine's Expository Dictionary of Biblical Words,* Merrill F. Unger, William White, ed., (Nashville: Thomas Nelson, 1985), in Biblesoft, *PC Study Bible,* v. 4.2, (Seattle: Biblesoft, 1988-2004).

3. Ibid.

Chapter 5: His Purpose Fulfilled

1. Job 3.

2. In pointing out these or any other temptations, I'm not saying that there aren't times when it is godly to act. What I am saying is that we have to be very careful about how we react to our afflictions. God has given us righteous ways of dealing with problems, and it's never wrong for us to use them. After all, Paul told believing slaves that if they could obtain their freedom, they should (1 Cor. 7:21). But there are also unrighteous ways of responding to affliction and sin. In short, we must never sin to accomplish some higher good.

3. God is the First Cause of everything that happens. He sovereignly rules and overrules in every circumstance. But there are second causes: people, including ourselves, and Satan. God is ruling, but He is also holding each person accountable for his or her actions. This is called concurrence and is taught forcefully in Scripture. He's the First Cause of everything that happens, but people or Satan are the proximate cause and will be held responsible for every evil action.

4. It seems to me that sometimes the worst counsel comes to us through our friends. I do believe that their motivation is to help and encourage us, but we would be wise to filter everything they advise us through the Word. Of course, we're to do that at all times. I think that we should be particularly careful about what those we trust tell us.

5. The Bible tells us that once David realized his sin, he confessed his folly to his followers. " 'The LORD forbid that I should do this thing to my

lord, the LORD's anointed, to put out my hand against him, seeing he is the Lord's anointed.' So David persuaded his men with these words and did not permit them to attack Saul" (1 Sam. 24:6–7 ESV).

6. We also pray because we've been commanded to do so and because God uses means (and prayer is one of those means) to accomplish the purposes that He has already foreordained will come to pass.

7. I'm not saying that God doesn't, at times and for His glory, ordain that we struggle with sin. After all, if He didn't ordain this struggle, it wouldn't happen. What I am saying is that we will never fall utterly or completely from His grace if we're truly His. We must always assume that it's His will that we humbly obey every command of His, but at the end of the day, we'll know what His secret will was for that day, because it will be what has happened.

8. Herbert Lockyer Sr., ed., *Nelson's Illustrated Bible Dictionary* (Nashville: Thomas Nelson, 1986 in Biblesoft, *PC Study Bible*, version 4.2b, (Seattle: Biblesoft, 1988–2004).

Chapter 6: Our Hearts Grow Strong

1. Jean Guichard is my favorite lighthouse photographer. He has a number of wonderful prints and calendars that I recommend.

2. W. E. Vine, *Vine's Expository Dictionary of Biblical Words*, Merrill F. Unger, William White, ed., (Nashville: Thomas Nelson, 1985), in Biblesoft, *PC Study Bible*, v. 4.2, (Seattle: Biblesoft, 1988-2004).

3. "And He found in the temple those who were selling oxen and sheep and doves, and the money changers seated at their tables. And He made a scourge of cords, and drove them all out of the temple, with the sheep and the oxen; and He poured out the coins of the money changers and overturned their tables; and to those who were selling the doves He said, 'Take these things away; stop making My Father's house a place of business.' His disciples remembered that it was written, 'Zeal for Your house will consume me' " (John 2:14–17).

"And Jesus entered the temple and drove out all those who were buying and selling in the temple, and overturned the tables of the money changers and the seats of those who were selling doves. And He said to them, 'It is written, "My house shall be called a house of prayer"; but you are making it a robbers' den' " (Matt 21:12–13).

4. B. B. Warfield, "The Emotional Life of Our Lord," an essay in his collected works, *Person and Work of Christ* (Phillipsburg, N.J.: P&R, 1970), 115, 117. "It is lexically inexcusable to reduce this emotional upset to the effects of empathy, grief, pain or the like" (D. A. Carson, *The Gospel According to John* [Grand Rapids: Eerdmans, 1991], 415.

5. John Calvin, *Harmony of the Evangelists,* trans. William Pringle, vols. (Grand Rapids: Eerdmans, 1949), 2:454.

6. Ibid.

7. Matthew Henry, *Matthew Henry's Commentary on the Whole Bible* (Peabody, Mass: Hendrickson, 1991) in Biblesoft, *PC Study Bible*, v. 4.2 (Seattle: Biblesoft, 1988–2004).

8. C. S. Lewis, *The Magician's Nephew* (New York: Harper Trophy, 2002), 141.

9. C. H. Spurgeon, *The Treasury of David,* accessed at http://www.spurgeon.org/treasury/ps057.htm, May 5, 2006.

10. Henry Wadsworth Longfellow, *The Lighthouse* (Library of America, 2000), 131. Accessed at http://www.poetry-online.org/longfellow_lighthouse.htm, May 5, 2006

Chapter 7: My Whole Heart Sings!

1. "('osher kabowd) person, self, glory, that is, the self or inner person (*Dictionary of Biblical Languages with Semantic Domains: Aramaic*; Libronix Digital Library). This Hebrew word translated "glory" in the ESV is translated "soul" in NIV.

2. Matthew Henry, *Matthew Henry's Commentary on the Whole Bible* (Peabody, Mass: Hendrickson, 1991) in Biblesoft, *PC Study Bible*, v. 4.2 (Seattle: Biblesoft, 1988–2004).

3. Dennis E. Johnson, *Let's Study Acts* (Carlisle, Pa.: Banner of Truth Trust, 2003), 207.

4. Ibid.

5. Jonathan Edwards, *Religious Affections: A Christian's Character Before God,* ed. James M. Houston (Minneapolis: Bethany House, 1996), 36.

6. A. W. Tozer, *Whatever Happened to Worship: A Call to True Worship* (Camp Hill, Pa.: Christian Publications, 1985), 13.

7. C. H. Spurgeon, *Charles Spurgeon on Prayer: A Thirty-Day Devotional Treasury,* ed. Lance Wubbles (Lynwood, Wash.: Emerald Books, 1998), day 13.

8. I'm not saying that God is unable or unwilling to perform miracles today. I do believe that God can and sometimes does bring miraculous deliverances to His people for all the reasons I listed above. Even so, we must always pray, "Your will be done," and then believe that it will be; whether that means instantaneous deliverance, deliverance through ordinary means, or no earthly deliverance at all.

9. Matthew Henry, *Matthew Henry's Commentary on the Whole Bible* (Peabody, Mass: Hendrickson, 1991) in Biblesoft, *PC Study Bible,* v. 4.2 (Seattle: Biblesoft, 1988–2004).

10. How the God of eternity defines "quickly" and how we might define it may be different. All we can be sure of is that from the perspective of an eternity, our prayers are heard and answered "in a brief space of time, in haste."

11. See Isaiah 63:9; Exodus 3:7–9; Judges 10:16; Zechariah 2:8; Matthew 25:40; Acts 9:4; Hebrews 2:18; 4:15.

12. Richard Baxter, *A Christian Directory* (Morgan, Pa.: Soli Deo Gloria, 1996), 75.

13. Tozer, *Whatever Happened to Worship,* 11.

Chapter 8: Be Exalted, O God!

1. Lehman Strauss, *The Arrows of the Almighty,* accessed at http://www.bible.org/page.asp?page_id=3261, May 5, 2006.

2. There are a couple of glimpses of faith and hope before Job turns the corner, such as Job 10:12; 13:15.

3. William Henry Green, *Conflict and Triumph: The Argument of the Book of Job Unfolded* (Carlisle, Pa.: Banner of Truth Trust, 1999), 94.

4. Ibid., 100. Emphasis added.

5. John Calvin, *Heart Aflame: Daily Readings from Calvin on the Psalms* (Phillipsburg, N.J.: P&R, 1999), 141.

Elyse Fitzpatrick is the award-winning author of 11 books on practical Christianity including *Idols of the Heart: Learning to Long for God Alone* and *The Afternoon of Life*. She holds an M.A. in Biblical Counseling and, along with her husband, Phil, counsels in her church in Southern California. She is a frequent conference speaker and brings to her writing and speaking an intimate knowledge of the problems many women face in their daily lives. She is the mother of three and "Mimi" to six grandchildren. She can be reached through her website at www.elysefitzpatrick.com.

Steve and Vikki Cook have been writing praise and worship songs and serving local churches for over 20 years. Their songs have been published by Integrity Music, Maranatha! Music, Word Music and Sovereign Grace Ministries.

Among their best known songs are "Before The Throne of God Above," "I Will Glory In My Redeemer" and "Great Are You, Lord."

Steve and Vikki and their two daughters reside in Orlando, Florida and are based at Metro Life Church (a part of the Sovereign Grace family of churches)

Visit www.BeforeTheThroneMusic.com for more information on their music and ministry.

Other books by Elyse Fitzpatrick:
The Afternoon of Life
Finding Purpose and Joy in Midlife
0-87552-197-5
$12.99

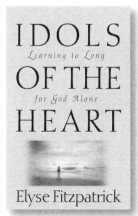

Idols of the Heart
Learning to Long for God Alone
0-87552-198-3
$13.99